THE ETHICS OF
MIGRATION RESEARCH
METHODOLOGY

THE ETHICS OF MIGRATION RESEARCH METHODOLOGY

DEALING WITH VULNERABLE IMMIGRANTS

EDITED BY

Ilse Van Liempt & Veronika Bilger

sussex
ACADEMIC
PRESS

BRIGHTON • PORTLAND

2 4 6 8 10 9 7 5 3 1

First published 2009 in Great Britain by
SUSSEX ACADEMIC PRESS
PO Box 139
Eastbourne BN24 9BP

and in the United States of America by
SUSSEX ACADEMIC PRESS
920 NE 58th Ave   Suite 300
Portland, Oregon 97213–3786

British Library Cataloguing in Publication Data
A CIP catalogue record for this book is available from the British Library.

Library of Congress Cataloging-in-Publication Data
The ethics of migration research methodology : dealing with vulnerable
   immigrants / edited by Ilse van Liempt and Veronika Bilger.
p. cm.
Includes bibliographical references and index.
ISBN 978-1-84519-331-7 (h/c : alk. paper)
1. Alien criminals—Research. 2. Immigrants—Moral and ethical aspects.
3. Emigration and immigration—Moral and ethical aspects. 4. Emigration
and immigration—Research. I. Van Liempt, Ilse. II. Bilger, Veronika.
HV6181.E84—2009
305.9′06912072—dc22

                                                                        2009018795

Mixed Sources
Product group from well-managed
forests and other controlled sources
www.fsc.org Cert no. SGS-COC-2482
© 1996 Forest Stewardship Council

Typeset and designed by SAP, Brighton & Eastbourne.
Printed by TJ International, Padstow, Cornwall.
This book is printed on acid-free paper.

Contents

CONTENTS

Preface and Acknowledgements

The idea of elaborating on methodological and ethical aspects when empirically working with migrants in precarious situations materialised during the joint work of researchers on an international project on 'Human smuggling and trafficking in migrants' (2002–2006). To this end three compatible research approaches were applied: document analysis (police files and court cases), expert interviews and narrative interviews with smuggled migrants. The collaborative work-style and the quest for sharing experiences resulted in the idea to launch a workshop on 'Human smuggling/trafficking seen from the inside' at the 9th International Metropolis Conference in Geneva 2004. The question addressed during this workshop was how the fields of smuggling, trafficking and irregular migration can be subject to research in a methodological and ethical sound way. Various research methods were discussed. In the course of the workshop it became obvious that there is in fact a strong need for a deepened debate on methodological aspects not only when researching human smuggling, trafficking and forms of irregularity but when in general involving migrants in various precarious situations.

Consequently, a follow-up workshop on 'interviewing vulnerable migrants for different reasons and with different purposes' was organised at the occasion of the 10th International Metropolis Conference in Toronto 2005. Both workshops confirmed that many researchers conducting research involving migrants in precarious situations in fact have similar questions and oftentimes feel like starting from scratch every time when attempting to find solutions for the methodological challenges they encounter. The idea of moving towards a collective publication on methodological aspects when researching with migrants in precarious situations finally materialised. We sincerely hope this book can be useful for researchers struggling with similar questions and for the training needs of students who wish to undertake research with special groups of people as it provides essential knowledge not only on the specific methodologies but also on ethical issues.

Introduction

Methodological and Ethical Concerns in Research with Vulnerable Migrants

VERONIKA BILGER AND ILSE VAN LIEMPT

R ecent changes in international migration towards more irregular patterns of migration (Global Commission on International Migration, 2005) have increased the number of 'vulnerable' migrants and have resulted in the emergence of important new fields for the study of migration. At the same time migration research is increasingly becoming a policy supporting research field. In this book we argue that both aspects; the growing political and legal marginalization of ever-larger immigrant populations and the increasing overlap of research and policy agendas have important methodological and ethical implications, which should be given more attention than was hitherto the case. As the concept of 'the vulnerable' is socially constructed a precise definition is problematic, but Moore & Miller (1999: 1034) contend that vulnerable individuals in general are people who 'lack the ability to make personal life choices, to make personal decisions, to maintain independence and to self-determine'. Vulnerable people will include the impoverished, disenfranchised, and/or those subject to discrimination, intolerance and/or stigma. Whatever definition of vulnerability we may use it is clear that extreme sensitivity is needed while conducting research with persons in vulnerable positions.

In our view, the increased attention given to research involving vulnerable persons has not yet been adequately translated into corresponding publications on methodological and ethical challenges in the study of migration. There are very few books that document and provide advice on how to go about performing sensitive research with vulnerable persons. The relative scarcity of these publications reflects on the one hand the dilemma of the multidisciplinary nature of the study of migration (see also Agozino 2000), which requires comprehensive knowledge and understanding of the methodological approaches of various disciplines. On the other hand the scarcity of publications on this topic may also reflect the reservations towards emphasizing the fact that there are serious dilemmas

1

related to empirical research especially with marginalised and vulnerable groups. Most research in the field of migration, and in particular in the field of refugees, has its origin in policy concerns (Black 2001). This has encouraged researchers to take the categories, concepts and priorities of policymakers at the core of their research design (Bakewell, 2008). This privileges the worldview of the policymakers in constructing the research, constraining the research questions asked, the subjects of study and the methodologies and analysis adopted. Criticising these underlying assumptions and reflecting on the consequences of this type of research is likely to bring more significant changes to the lives of migrants, as certain questions derived from policy priorities may produce results that would be harmful for the community. The delineation of the field by policy categories is not only a challenge for those studying migration but generally broader for policy-driven research (Minnery & Greenhalgh 2007).

So far only little attention has been paid to building a body of literature on qualitative approaches within migration research that would enable migration researchers to learn from one another. We rarely get information on the design of the research or the research processes such as how participants were identified and accessed, to what degree participants were involved in the research, how translation issues were handled etc. Even less insight is provided in regard to difficulties experienced, possible biases and the researchers' positioning. Consequently migration researchers working with vulnerable migrants are faced with similar questions time and again and often feel like reinventing the wheel when trying to find solutions for the challenges they encounter.

Is migration research unique?

Today migration is one of the most cross-disciplinary fields in academia allowing for interdisciplinary and methodological pluralism. Still, the field of migration is not unique in its approach(es) and methodological challenges. The multidisciplinary and at the same time topic-centred nature of migration studies bears the risk that the alleged or real specificities of this field of research or indeed commonalities which migration research shares with other research areas is not adequately reflected. Researchers in a variety of research fields have developed a sophisticated expertise in regard to all kinds of methodological and ethical concerns. Outside the 'migration field' there is excellent work addressing methodological issues and the question of research ethics from a wide range of perspectives that may apply to migration research as well. Still, the study of migration is shaped by specific features rooted in its very nature, with migrants representing the main type of actors and migrations the main type of processes. Nevertheless, not every group manifestation is to be explained by a single aspect (migration) alone. In reality, a broad range of factors that might only marginally be linked to a migration background might influence the views, perceptions or actions of migrants.

A specific challenge arises from the fact that in many cases various dimensions may overlap, influence or determine one another. In his introduction to 'Researching refugees: Lessons, challenges and ways forward' Bakewell highlights: 'the challenge for refugee researchers is how to hold in balance the recognition of the distinctive situation of the refugees and the underlying 'normality' of the people. It is too easy to draw on the fact that someone has experienced forced migration as an explanation for many observations in the field, which may equally apply to non-refugees' (Bakewell 2007: 8). In fact, his critique does not only apply to refugee research, but to all research involving migrants or their descendants. As a continuous task, researchers need to carefully weigh different factors according to their actual significance in order to avoid a 'migration bias'. More subject-centred approaches may be a useful tool in understanding these different factors. Moreover, the fact that the social environment of potential participants is very much shaped by particular institutional settings in the broader framework of migration policy and legislation has several basic ethical and methodological implications specific to migration research and especially to research involving migrants in precarious situations.

A first implication is that the researcher positions the envisaged research within this specific institutional framework. As a corollary, this positioning is reflected in the framing of the research design and the respective methodological approach. For example, institutions are particularly intrusive in regard to undocumented migration, illegal residence or other aspects of 'illegality'. They strongly shape migrants' lives by naturally setting a certain frame in which these migrants are able to navigate. As a consequence, the framing of research questions and methodological approaches shape the nature and level of involvement of participating persons. After all, in case of undocumented migration research outcomes might have a severe impact on the participants' current and future life if the research was not carefully designed. This, and similar aspects open a wide range of methodological questions as for example how to access these groups of persons and questions of professional ethics such as how to deal with confident information or minimize harm, as, after all, they might not see any good reason to participate and put their current lives at risk. **Part One** – *Methods and Ethics in Institutional S ettings* – presents two case studies on research with vulnerable migrants within the institution 'prison'.

The contributions in **Part Two** – *Rethinking Basic Research Methods* – base their primary focus on the questions of choosing the right methodological approach. By assessing various approaches authors elaborate on questions and strategies in regard to accessing and keeping contact with hard-to-reach-populations. Other questions are framed around building up trust in a setting with high levels of suspicion towards the researcher, collecting sensitive information, data processing and ethical dissemination of the results. The question on who would benefit from research and whether research may potentially cause harm to respondents are core issues in research involving vulnerable groups, most notably in commissioned research as in this case the topics and directions of research are already pre-defined by stakeholders.

Furthermore, qualitative research also allows for reflections on the role of the researcher in regard to the construction and production of knowledge. **Part Three** pays special attention to the role and position of the researcher within research with vulnerable migrants, thereby aiming at eventually disrupting the asymmetric power relations between the researcher and those researched. Sometimes it is argued that within advocacy and awareness-driven research certain aspects of social reality might remain under researched. One can however also argue that, as all research is framed in a certain context, the specific strength of advocacy-driven research is that it puts emphasis on considering the institutional frame and its effects on the creation of knowledge. Moreover, research can be called exploitative when the interest of the researchers alone guides every stage of the research process. Research that aims to give voice to the marginalised should try to transform these exploitative aspects of positivist science. One good example is the EU-funded project RIME (Releasing Indigenous Multiculturalism through Education) where the theory and practice of re-evaluation counselling was used in order to help participants to emotionally release hurtful experiences (van den Anker, 2006).

In migration research, and even more so in transnational migration research (Borkert & De Tona 2006), the question by whom research is carried out is particularly interesting when researchers (or part of the research team) are themselves migrants or even exponent of the population, community and/or identity group they are conducting studies with (Borkert & De Tona 2006). It becomes even more interesting when 'minority' researchers as 'outsiders' conduct research in the majority population which otherwise usually holds hegemony over the production of knowledge (Phoenix 1994: 55–56). Such reflections also have ethical consequences as 'qualitative methodologies allow us to question how the researcher's standpoint influences access to "the field", the relation of the researcher to the research participants and, the process of interpretation and data analysis' (De Tona 2006, par. 4). With regard to research involving vulnerable migrants there are two important questions to ask:

1   Why is the research conducted and why is it conducted in this specific way? As elaborated above, ethical questions in research

start with framing the research. Why is the research conducted and what is the researcher's position vis-à-vis the participants? Subsequently, such basic theoretical reflections find their translation into respective methodological approaches.

2   How is the research conducted? On the level of the research process itself, there are different ethical questions affecting methodological questions and vice versa. These questions circulate around questions concerning where and how will I get access to vulnerable research participants and how will I negotiate access? How should I conduct research which is sensitive? What ethical considerations do I need to observe? What is my role as a researcher in relation to the researched? How do I represent their views and how is the quality and content of the data collected affected by participants' vulnerable position? And finally how do I present the findings to the public?

In the following, we discuss some contributions of selected research traditions to debates on methodological and ethical issues both within migration research and beyond which are regarded relevant to our case studies as presented in this collective book. Although not all of the research traditions deal with marginalised or vulnerable groups, they all have important lessons to teach in regard to both ethical and methodological issues and the link between them.

Research on forced migration and the fine line between researchers and practitioners

Social science research on forced migration initially emerged within the framework of policy-oriented research in refugee situations in the 'developing world'. In this context, methodological and ethical issues arising in research on forced migration were often structurally similar to issues refugee agencies, relief workers and government officials were confronted with. In particular camp-like situations and humanitarian emergencies provided a favourable environment for engaging in methodological and ethical debates and reflecting on the research process itself (see Bloch 1999, Jacobsen & Landau 2003). Research that focused exclusively on 'methodological' problems as experienced by practitioners rather than researchers (e.g. Kibreab, 2004) provides important insights that have direct implications for research methodologies and ethics. After all, the position of a researcher vis-à-vis refugees may not be so different from that of a humanitarian fieldworker (see Shuman & Bohmer 2004, Salis Gross 2004). Both are placed within a specific institutional frame that labels identities (Zetter 1991), shapes behaviour, attitudes, opinions, and public personae of refugees as well as their responses to questions. Indeed, from the perspective of refugees, a researcher may appear to be just as much part of the institutional structures dealing with refugees as are government officials and aid workers (see Harrell-Bond 1986, Barsky 1994, Hynes 2003).

A specific ethical challenge that is not peculiar to research on asylum seekers per se but which is perhaps more pressing there than in other areas of research concerns the role of advocacy in the research process. Very often advocacy-driven research runs the danger of overstating or indeed, misrepresenting research findings, or, as Jacobsen & Landau (2003) phrase it, of 'talking crisis', in order to achieve certain political outcomes. Conversely, findings that highlight, for example, how asylum applicants adjust (e.g. by adapting life stories etc.) to the expectations of actors within the asylum system, pose questions as to the potential negative consequences of such research both for individuals and groups at large. Indeed, in the field of refugee studies a lot has been done in regard to advance methodological and ethical sensitivity. Increasingly, also important outlets in this field for example the Journal for Refugee Studies, the UNHCR series New issues in Refugee Research or the Refugee Survey Quarterly and others regularly present case studies reflecting such challenges and more broadly cover aspects of developing methodology and research ethics in this field.

Feminist approaches and community based methodologies

As for other research fields important contributions to the debates on ethics and methodology is provided by feminist scholars. Feminist research differs from other types of research mostly by its worldview as it is women and their concerns which are the focus of investigation. A clear intention is to undertake research which is beneficial for women and not just about women. The concern of feminist research is to construct knowledge that 'writes women into history' and acknowledges their active roles. Advocating for 'agency' by recognizing participants as the experts on their own experiences feminist researchers have also pointed to ethical dilemmas in established theoretical and methodological approaches. This concerns the understanding of subjectivity as well as power relations between the researcher and the research subjects. Feminist approaches actively seek to remove the power imbalance between researcher and participants and, by doing so, to challenge the established understanding of knowledge production and ownership of knowledge not exclusively 'owned' by the researcher (Harding 1987, Wolf, 1996). As a corollary, feminist scholars have challenged not only quantitative research, but also qualitative research approaches and have experimented with and promoted the use of ethnographic research such as life histories, in-depth interviews, participatory research and community-based methodologies which allow to relate to participants 'in subjective way on their term rather than in objective ways on the researchers' term' (Edwards 1990: 489). Although 'ethnographic research has enjoyed a long and valued place within immigration studies (. . .) feminist ethnographic enquiry tends to focus (. . .) on the perspectives and understandings of subjects' actions and beliefs, thus facilitating the definition of potential interventions that reflect and respect local knowledge' (Mahler & Pessar 2006: 30).

The researcher herself also received a lot of attention in feminist research as feminist research breaks the silence about researchers' own experiences of dealing with emotions. Feminist research admits that researchers who are caught in emotionally laden research should not only look at the impact of their research at participants but also at themselves. Moreover feminist researchers explicitly admit that research is personal as well as political. Promoted by politically motivated feminist research this perspective of reciprocal understanding of research processes with its basic aim to eventually change social inequalities by recognising and placing standpoints of structurally marginalised groups of persons is no longer exclusively limited to gender-related questions within migration studies. It has found its way into the broader theoretical and methodological framework especially when it comes to questions on how societal structures and institutions shape and impact migrants' lives and their strategies to cope with it. This is maybe also why feminist research has contributed a lot to refugee and asylum research (see for example Temple & Moran 2006).

Another area in the research on gender and migration of specific relevance to this book are contributions to the research field of migrant sexwork and migrant sexworkers and related topics such as, gender and labour migration, forced labour and human trafficking (see for example Kempadoo & Doezema 1998, Wijers & Lap-Chew 1996, Andrijasevic 2003 and Dahinden & Efionayi-Mäder in this book). The highly controversial discussion also within feminist research on migrant sexwork and human trafficking serve as good example for difficulties arising from the lack of clear theoretical concepts, definitions, terms and categories. The controversial debate on migrant prostitution and 'human trafficking for the purpose of sexual exploitation' still is and will continue to be intensely discussed as it conflates around unresolved positions on the issues of female migration, prostitution/sexwork and agency. The interpretations of the underlying definitions vary significantly among researchers themselves as they also reflect the researchers' political, moral and ethical stance towards the general question of especially (migrant) women's participation in the sex business in general.

Research dealing with 'hard-to-reach' populations

Another research field increasingly raising and sharing particularly methodological concerns in the field of migration are those involving the so-called 'hidden' or 'hard-to-reach' populations (Atkinson & Flint 2001, Duncan et al. 2003). These populations are said to be hidden or hard-to-reach because they are hidden from the point of view of sampling and as such difficult to find. 'Hidden' or 'hard-to-reach' populations may also actively try to conceal their identity as belonging to that group what makes it even more difficult to find them. Examples of these populations are drug users, the mentally and chronically ill, sexually active teens, persons with eating disorders or gays and lesbians. The problem with these terms is that they are stigmatizing as 'it defines the problem as one within the group itself not within your approach to them' (Smith 2006).

In regard to migration, examples are expressed in case studies on undocumented smuggled or trafficked migrants. Empirical studies on 'hidden' or 'hard-to-reach' populations necessarily call for approaches different from those commonly used for research on more easily observable populations. By definition, size and location of these populations are unknown, thus difficulties in sampling and in applying quantitative methods of collecting and extrapolating data are inevitable (see Jandl 2004, Vogel 2002, Engbersen et al. 2002).

Authors in this field often reflect on established techniques of locating and accessing hard-to-reach-populations and, similar to research in forced migrations and asylum seekers, on issues of trust and mistrust (see for example Cornelius 1982, Ellis & MacGaffey 1996). In addition very often 'there exists a strong privacy concern when it comes to 'hard-to-reach' populations. Membership may involve stigmatised or illegal behaviour leading individuals to refuse to cooperate, or give unreliable answers to protect their privacy' (Heckathorn 1997: 174). This concern touches upon another challenging aspect namely the quality of data and information collected and it's processing. Most challenging in this field, and very controversial ever since it is discussed, is the undercover, covert approach to fieldwork. Although exposed to ethical criticism 'it remains a method of choice for social scientists who fear that by openly announcing their intentions, they will cause potential subjects to scurry' (Herrera 2003: 315).

Research dealing with 'deviant behaviour'

In research on organised criminal activities and 'deviant behaviour' the challenge of how to get information becomes specifically evident as 'typical tools of the criminologist – observation, surveys, interviews, samples and questionnaires – are either extremely difficult or even impossible to use' (Finckenauer & Waring 1998: 7). In addition, the development of research questions may not only require the thorough consideration of individuals' perceptions but also the examination of group identities and their under-lining values, norms and constructions of meanings. The way researchers interpret their role vis-à-vis their individual respondents and the groups they are representing is therefore of crucial importance (Hobbs 2001).

In response to a more general linkage between migration, security and crime that has shaped public debates on migration in industrialised coun-tries since the 1990s, the area of research on 'deviant behaviour' gains increasing relevance. For a variety of reasons the share of incarcerated non-nationals has significantly risen in recent years (see Barsky in this book). This situation has gained increasing prominence in various disciplines, ranging from anthropology, sociology of law to criminology and political science (see for example the 'EU foreign prisoners project').[1] Recently, selected studies have analyzed policies and enforcement actions, immi-grants' specific vulnerability to restrictive treatment in the criminal justice system, exclusionary characteristics, its implications for rehabilitation processes, the implications of an increasingly diverse inmate population, and new challenges for governance of a multicultural prison-life. While in this case the target group might theoretically be easier to access we will raise attention in **Part One** to the fact that the characteristics of the insti-tution 'prison' raise very particular ethical and methodological concerns.

Discourse and conversational analysis

Another research field that has made important contributions to qualita-tive research methodologies is the discourse and conversational analysis with the related field of 'intercultural communication'. This field of research emerged from different linguistic and sociological traditions and has undergone an exceptional growth in the past two decades. It attempts to deconstruct the meanings participants have about their lived experi-ences and the language they use. Discourse analysis has replaced the observation that an 'objective reality exists' with a view that reality is 'chaotic and unknowable' (Grbich 2004). Objectivity is replaced by reflexive subjectivity and the politics of position. In this line of reasoning meanings become recognised as individual creations which require inter-pretation and negotiation. Research on communication strategies has highlighted the challenges in dealing with differences in the understanding and conceptualization of communication situations, as well as differences in the understanding of the concepts about which persons of different backgrounds converse (see Ehlich 1998, Gumperz & Roberts 1991, Hartog 2006).

Critical discourse analysts have also highlighted the potential for misunderstandings produced by highly formalised and asymmetric communication situations. Research in this field has therefore provided valuable insights into power asymmetries and power dynamics at play in various formalised communication situations such as in medical examinations between health workers and patients, in court situations before defendants and professionals, or in class rooms between teachers and students (see Harris 1995, Trosberg 1995, Wodak 1985). As such this research field has provided important insights for conducting research in institutionalised settings as it points out the importance of self-reflexivity on the side of the researcher as well as permits the voices of the 'Other' and their reflexive practices. The assumption often is that once research begins participants will cooperate and freely tell researchers what they want to know. But why should people, and especially the ones who are already vulnerable, tell the truth? Researchers are in that case naturally viewed with suspicion and researchers have to find ways to 'gain access' to their subjects (see also Bilger & van Liempt in this book).

When researching (with) immigrants difficulties in communication might be reinforced by basic methodological challenges such as for example the need to deal with various languages. Especially refugee studies and the research fields dealing with health issues thereby explicitly refer to challenges that go beyond simple linguistic difficulties by pointing to the fact that differences of meaning of key-terms as – e.g. in the area of health different concepts of well-being – need to be taken into account (see for example Salis Gross 2004). This becomes most apparent in all areas where a metaphorical language is used and explains the importance for carefully selecting interpreters and take into consideration difficulties and limits of certain methods of analysis (see for example Temple et al. 2006). However, another dimension to the role of interpreters appears when interpreters from the same ethnic, linguistic or cultural background are involved in order to ease building up trust. Especially in institutional contexts, such as – in the context of this book – the asylum system or prison, a person with a presumed 'insider' position might not be trusted exactly because of this position (see Shuman & Bohmer 2004, Doornbos 2003).

Standardised ethical principles and the dilemma of 'how to do it right'

For a long time ethical issues relating to research that involves human subjects were limited to the field of medical studies and related subjects such as human anthropology. Ethical standards in social science are much more recent. The first international code of ethics to protect the right of people from research abuse was conducted in 1949 in the Nuremberg

Code. Other Codes of Ethics are the 'Declaration of Helsinki' (1964) and the 'Belmont Report' (1978). Today, in many countries social science research is routinely assessed in respect to its ethical implications. Ethic principles are integrated in a variety of national guidelines and regulations and, especially in the Anglo-Saxon countries, ethic committees are set up to which researchers should hand in their projects for approval. More recently, responding to the increase in transnational research partnerships and new developments in information technologies multiplying the sources of information available, which increasingly also raise issues of authenticity, verifiability and research quality, the European Commission explicitly commissioned the RESPECT-project with the aim to develop standards for socio-economic research in the European Union. The Project RESPECT has developed a Code of Conduct for conducting research in the social sciences based on a synthesis of the contents of a large number of various existing professional and ethical codes of practice (see www.respectproject.org). The result of the project, the 'EU Code of Ethics for socio-economic research' distinguishes three main types of ethical responsibility of researchers: responsibility to society, professional expertise and standards and responsibilities to research participants. This opens a wide range of questions when conducting research involving vulnerable migrants. To decide on what would benefit society is specifically peculiar in policy-oriented research and, even more so, research commissioned by policy makers or other relevant stakeholders simply because the broader framework of migration policy and legislation sets the frame in which these migrants move. On the individual level of participation researchers and participants might not necessarily access the harms and benefits of a research in the same way. Hence, to conceive the views of the potential or actual participants from their point of view may be a very complex undertaking. In general research ethics is often more about institutional and professional regulations and codes of conduct than it is about the needs, aspirations or worldviews of 'vulnerable communities' (Smith 2005: 96).

Ethical standards in social science are based on three basic principles: respect for human dignity, justice and beneficence. The standards also emphasise four guidelines through which these principles should be applied: informed consent, non-deception, privacy and confidentiality, and accuracy (Christians 2005: 144). These standards and ethical assessment procedures however still bear the hallmarks of medical research and life sciences and do not respond to certain areas of social sciences. The criteria of informed consent, non-deception, privacy and confidentiality for example seem not to be much of an issue to research where there is a reciprocal relation between the researcher and the researched. In his review Clifford Christians points to the radical break social and feminist thinkers have made with previous ideas surrounding research ethics based on the epistemological critique of positivist thinking and its norm of objectivity:

'Rather than searching for neutral principles to which all parties can appeal, social ethics rests on a complex view of moral judgements as integrating into an organic whole various perspectives – everyday experience, beliefs about the good, and feelings of approval and shame – in terms of human relations and social structures' (Christians 2005: 149). Christians argues that 'research methodologies that have broken down the walls between subject and researchers ought to be excluded from IRB's oversight, because they cannot meet the old criteria' (Christians 2005: 157).

In research which enables people to come to terms with their everyday experiences and which understands research subjects as participating agents carrying knowledge and interpreting their own life worlds, ethical concerns of justice, fairness and moral actions go far beyond rigid sets of rules and guidelines. Elements such as moral values, ideals, personal and professional standards, empathy or intuition all play an important part in these research projects. Ethical codes however are very general and absolute. According to De Lain they are 'intellectualized, objective constructions that make no allowance for cultural, social, personal and emotional variations' (De Lain 2000: 4). Most research, especially with vulnerable people, raises much wider questions of power relations, equality and subjectivity. Informed consent for example is defined as the provision of information to participants about the purpose of the research, its procedures, potential risks, benefits and alternatives. The principle of voluntary participation from an informed position bears specific difficulties when participants find themselves in vulnerable positions. In regard to migrants here again the broader framework of policy and legislation provides a specific dimension to these principles. As laws, regulations and measures which shape participants' lives are often not fully transparent; participants may not easily appraise the possible consequences upon their lives and strategies. Language and cultural factors may also affect people's understanding of what participation in a research project means and in what way it could harm or benefit them. As Augustin (2008) argues 'the version of ethics that is usually referred to in research is, like so much else, a thoroughly western one'.

Another concern in this regard is deception. Although a highly contested methodological approach researchers may decide for 'covert' participant observation especially in research with 'hidden' or 'hard-to-reach' populations (see Markova in this book). When dealing with confidentiality and anonymity the issue arises that insensitive treatment could not only harm individuals, but a group of persons or a community as a whole. If the necessary sensitivity in this regard is not shown from the researchers' side the consequences for the respondents might be far-reaching, in some cases even life threatening. Qualitative research in more sensitive areas usually demands a more active involvement of researchers. In some cases researchers have to be aware of the fact that obtaining certain information would automatically turn them into 'bearers of secrets' being in possession of information that could prove to be very harmful for the respondents, sometimes without even being aware of this. On the other hand there is the issue of reciprocity. Traditional methodology text books advise against offering assistance to respondents. But the moral implications of this have been challenged by social and feminist thinkers[2] who do not only insist on the principle of mutual benefit but believe that rejection of requested help may 'harm' participants (see also Markova and Staring in this book). Moreover, ethical questions are not static. They need to be raised and reflected from the beginning of conceptualising the research until placing the results in the public arena (see for example Glazer 1982). Muller & Bell (2002) likewise argue that ethics are often considered an 'after-thought' or something that needs to be considered only at the moment when the research proposal is evaluated by the ethical committee, whereas they need to constitute an ongoing part of research and should take part before, during and after the research. Thus understanding ethics as a process rather than a rigid set of moral values to be applied proposes a different way of obtaining informed consent that is well accommodated within the flexible nature of qualitative methodology.

To conclude, ethical standards may provide a useful general frame of reference. Nevertheless, its formalistic recommendations are of limited use as a guideline for the difficult choices and decisions to be made at different stages of the research process. Recently published books, such as Mauthner et al. (2002) address the gap between research practice and ethical principles. Increasingly researchers critically report their own experiences when conducting research in specific fields or groups while struggling with the fact that in the research practice of qualitative research, ethical codes often do not give an adequate answer on 'how to do it right'. The 'EU Code of Ethics for socio-economic research' as developed by the RESPECT-project takes the pronounced critique on standardised principles into account not only by referring to it in the introductory part, but also throughout the report by including a section on possible 'dilemmas that may need to be addressed' associating every single principle. Still, by pointing to Friedmann et al. (2002) the RESPECT-report highlights that ethical codes 'enable professionals to make informed choices when faced with an ethical dilemma, so if they behave unethically they do so by design rather than by error' (Dench, Iphofen & Huws 2004: 31).

Next to this newly developed EU Code of Ethics for socio-economic research, there is in fact an ever-growing demand for addressing ethical and methodological challenges when researching persons in precarious situations and/or specific institutional settings. The 'Ethical Guidelines for Good Research practice' in the field of forced migration studies[2] serve as one example for the attempt to acknowledge the specific challenges for the research process imposed by the fact that 'research on forced migration occurs in many places around the world; some where they are "at home" and others where they are in some way "foreign" and the subsequent consequence that resulting studies occur within a variety of economic, cultural, legal and political settings' necessitating specific sensitivity' (RSQ 2007: 163). The multifaceted nature of empirical problems would suggest multidisciplinary approaches and at the very least, that migration researchers take on board insights won by other researchers working in one of the fields dealing with marginalised populations. However until now not so many of these discussions have found their way into the broader frame of migration research. The Forum: Qualitative Research for example initialised an electronic debate on Qualitative Research and Ethics, an exchange and information tool directed to social researchers and participants alike aiming at contributing to a deliberate investigation of all possible topics relating to ethics in qualitative research (http://www.qualitative-research.net). Only few however are to be found on migration related issues. From our point of view a fruitful avenue for future research therefore, is to explore common methodological approaches across disciplines and across subject areas in a more systematic and comprehensive way. Against this background, we think that the present collection of methodological and ethical difficulties and considerations of those researchers who had joined together and started a discussion on these matters at the International Metropolis Conferences in the years 2004 and 2005 and afterwards contributes to a much needed broader discussion on methodological and ethical developments in the field of migration and a step forwards on our way to better understand on 'how to do it right'.

Contributions to this book

In the following chapters we will deal with all of the above-mentioned aspects. In some parts of the book more emphasis is put on difficulties in regard to methodological approaches while other parts link these difficulties to ethical questions more explicitly. Some of the presented research faced similar difficulties but applied different strategies to deal with these difficulties, while others deal with the same group of participants or similar topics but face very different challenges. What is common to all contributions is that in all case studies the participating migrants find themselves multiply marginalised and in very vulnerable situations. Therefore all case studies presented touch upon various aspects of the above-presented debates even though their primary focus lies on specific parts. Due to this specific type of marginalization and vulnerability it seems imperative that all contributions take into account the political and legal frameworks

governing their participants' lives. Difficulties in accessing potential participants, building up trust in a context of mistrust, the role of the researcher
vis-à-vis research participants, dealing with confident information etc. are
the basic issues guiding all contributions.

The common aim of the case studies presented is to critically reflect
possibilities and limitations when conducting research involving migrants
in vulnerable positions from various perspectives. The contributions very
openly reflect on specific difficulties and possible mistakes that have
occurred in the beginning of conceptualising the research, on the limits and
reasoning behind modifications of research techniques and approaches
and questions connected to dissemination of research findings. With this
book we take the possibility to continue our reflections on 'how to do it
right' or at least on 'how to do it better' we had started already in 2004. We
believe that the 'lessons learned' by others who had to go through this
process already, are suited to contribute fruitfully to the design of new
research that will have to deal with similar challenges. The book is split in
three parts: (1) methodology and ethics in institutional settings, (2)
rethinking basic research methods, and (3) the role of the researcher when
dealing with migrants in precarious situations.

Part One: Methods and Ethics in Institutional Settings

In the first part, methods and ethics in institutional settings the primary
focus is on methodological problems and ethical concerns when
conducting research on migration issues in a context where the political
and institutional framework poses very concrete methodological and
ethical questions, namely the institution 'prison'.

Prof. Robert F. Barsky (Vanderbilt University, Nashville, Tennessee, United States) *Methodological issues for the study of migrant incarceration in an era of discretion in law in the southern USA.*

Based on insights into the framework of a changing immigration policy
practise and more specifically of immigrant incarceration since the adoption of new post-9/11 legislation Robert Barsky shows that within the
context of heightened security and high level of discretion a whole new
definition of the term 'vulnerable population' is created specifically
applying to non-citizens. Based on these insights he presents the outlines
of an interview-based methodology for a research project in this specific
field. Exploring officials' and incarcerated persons' expertise on changed
administrative practises of incarceration by conducting interviews insight
the institution 'prison' is subject to several constraints and difficulties. It

makes it difficult for researchers who need to get past both the Institution Review Board Guidelines concerning vulnerable populations as well as the ever-stringent policies regulating prisoners. Barsky provides material for this kind of work within and beyond the United States, because even though some of the practices are particular to the US context similar developments can be observed in other countries as well.

Dr. Christin Achermann (Swiss Forum for Migration and Population Studies, (SFMS), Geneva, Switzerland) *Multi-perspective research on foreigners in prisons in Switzerland*

Similarly, in her contribution Christin Achermann highlights that 'prisons are special places, with their own logic and rules and full of ambiguity – for inmates, staff and also researchers'. Achermann takes on a different focus by exploring the situation of the immigrant inmate population in Swiss prisons and how various actors in the field assess this situation. Taking into account different views and assessments not only has methodological advantages but is also informed by ethical considerations. Giving equally voice to various views and valuing expertise from all persons involved (migrants, staff and administration) is one way of complying with the ethical principle of respect and responsibility to society. This also involves a certain level of reflection on the role of the researcher vis-à-vis its respondents as the question of justice and injustice play an inevitable role when researching in the institution prison. Based on this reflection in her concluding section she provides recommendations on what she 'would change if conducting a similar research'.

Part Two: Rethinking Basic Research Methods

The contributions in the second part rethinking basic research methods base their primary focus on the questions of choosing the right methodological approach. By assessing various approaches authors elaborate on questions and strategies especially in regard to accessing hard-to-reach-populations, collecting information, data processing and dissemination of results.

Dr. Richard Staring (The Erasmus University, Rotterdam, the Netherlands) *Different methods to research irregular migration*

Richard Staring provides insight into methodological issues when researching in a group not easily accessible. In his contribution he reflects on his research on processes of irregular migration of undocumented

Turkish immigrants in the Netherlands and his experience with applying two methodological approaches namely ethnographic research and document analysis (police files). He elaborates on different forms of selectivity in both research approaches and concludes that still, depending on the specific research question, both research methods – on-site ethnographic research and secondary analysis of closed criminal investigations – can be successfully deployed in answering questions on the irregular migration processes and the supporting social capital.

Prof. Janine Dahinden and Denise Efionayi-Mäder (Swiss Forum for Migration and Population Studies (SFMS), Geneva, Switzerland) *Challenges and strategies in empirical fieldwork with asylum seekers and migrant sex workers.*

Janine Dahinden and Denise Efionayi-Mäder take another perspective by reflecting on concrete methodological and ethical challenges they were confronted with both in a research on asylum seekers and in a study on migrant sex-workers. They decidedly take position by giving voice to structurally marginalised groups of persons. Having conducted interviews in both studies Dahinden and Efionayi-Mäder specifically focus on how best to access potential interview partners and they reflect on the quality of the data they collected in both studies. They also point at the broader ethical concern researchers are inevitably faced with when involving migrants in precarious situations by dealing with politically, socially, morally and legally controversially assessed topics.

Veronika Bilger and Dr. Ilse van Liempt (International Centre for Migration and Policy Development (ICMPD), Vienna, Austria and Sussex Centre for Migration Research (SCMR), Brighton, United Kingdom) *Methodological and ethical dilemmas in research among smuggled migrants.*

The last contribution in **Part Two** is based on experiences from a collaborative research project on human smuggling. Veronika Bilger and Ilse van Liempt argue that already in the beginning ethical issues may be beyond the control of researchers as professional review boards themselves are in a powerful position to set the terms for selecting the appropriate methodological approach based on their perspective of who has a say and who does not, who can provide knowledge and who can not. Migrants' who had been smuggled were assumed to be incapable of providing insights into the social organisation of human smuggling. Against such doubts the research team however insisted in the decision to include migrants' expertise by conducting qualitative interviews. Still Bilger and van Liempt highlight that conducting and analysing the interviews proved to be the most challenging part in the course of the project. In their contribution they touch upon issues of accessing potential participants, how to build up trust in a context of mistrust, how narrations might be influenced by 'external' structures factors such as migration experience, migration policies and administrations, smugglers or the migrant community. Bilger and van Liempt conclude that the results of the research challenged common wisdom in approaching human smuggling exactly because a voice was given to otherwise underrepresented individuals.

Part Three: The Role of the Researcher when dealing with migrants in precarious situations

What is common to all contributions in the third part of this book is the reflection over the role of the researcher from various perspectives when researching migrants in precarious situations. Attention will be paid to the insider–outsider debate as well as to the close link between advocacy and research in this particular field.

Dr. Eugenia Markova (Working Lives Research Institute at London Metropolitan University, London, United Kingdom)
The 'insider' position: ethical dilemmas and methodological concerns in researching undocumented migrants with the same ethnic background.

Eugenia Markova who conducted research on the (informal) labour market performance of undocumented Bulgarian immigrants in three European countries elaborates on what a difference the position of being an 'outsider' or 'insider' makes. Markova argues that at first hand her active engagement with the Bulgarian community opened way to undocumented co-nationals participating in her research and eased access to important locations and information. Still, being a co-national, part of the community and therefore a friend opens a range of difficulties in the handling over conflicting roles. As she states: 'clearly, this experience can be classified as "covert" research'. While researchers always hope to establish at trustworthy relationship with their respondents the situation looks slightly different if this relationship is already established beforehand. She argues that although using friendship for obtaining information might be considered a form of deception, some insights, especially when illegal activities are involved, cannot be gained by using conventional open methods but inevitably require certain 'social lies'.

Nuria Empez (PhD student at Max-Planck Institute for Demographic Research, Rostock, Germany) *The fieldworker as social worker: dilemmas in research with Morrocan unaccompanied minors in Spain*

In her research Nuria Empez follows Moroccan unaccompanied minors in their migration process from their home country Morocco to their destination Spain. Research involving children, considered as one of the most vulnerable groups, already bears specific issues in regard to methodology and research ethics. The fact that these children are staying undocumented only adds to their vulnerability. In addition, as these children organise their lives in the Spanish streets and thus constantly move bears additional peculiarities to be handled especially in regard to accessing these children and, as they usually organise in groups, establishing trust. As a researcher and at the same time a social worker, Empez highlights on advantages when navigating the fine line between these roles.

Notes

1   The EU Foreign prisoners project, coordinated by Professor Anton van Kalmthout and Femke Hofstee-van der Meulen from Tilburg University (The Netherlands) 'addresses the issue of social exclusion of prisoners who are detained in the EU outside their country of origin' in 25 EU Member States (http://www.foreignersinprison.eu)

2   Presented by the Refugee Studies Centre in 2007 and adapted from the ethical guidelines of the Association of Social Anthropologists of the Commonwealth.

Bibliography

Agozino, B. (eds.) (2000), *Theoretical and Methodological Issues in Migration Research: Interdisciplinary, Intergenerational and International Perspectives*, Aldershot: Ashgate.

Andrijasevic, R. (2003), 'The Difference Borders Make: (Il) legality, Migration and Trafficking in Italy among Eastern European Women in Prostitution', in S. Ahmed, C. Castaneda, A. Fortier & M. Sheller (eds.), *Uprootings/ Regroundings: Questions of Home and Migration*: 251–272. Oxford: Berg.

Anker, van den (2006), 'Re-evaluation Counselling as a tool in combating ethnic discrimination and xenophobia', in: van den Anker & Apostolov (eds.), *Educating for Peace and Multiculturalism. A handbook for trainers*: 81–89. The University of Warwick.

Atkinson, R. & J. Flint (2001), 'Accessing hidden and hard-to-reach populations: Snowball research strategies', *Social Research Update*, 33.

Augustin, L. (2008), Border Thinking on Migration, Culture, Economy and Sex: http://www.nodo50.org/Laura_Augustin

Bakewell, O. (2008), 'Research Beyond the Categories: The Importance of Policy Irrelevant Research into Forced Migration', *Journal of Refugee Studies*, Vol. 21 (4): 432–453.

Bakewell, O. (2007), Researching Refugees: Lessons from the past, current challenges and future directions, *Refugee Survey Quarterly*, Vol. 26 (3): 6–14.

Barsky R.F. (1994), *Constructing a Productive Other: Discourse theory and the Convention Refugee Hearings*. Philadelphia: John Benjamins Publishing Company.

Black, R. (2001), 'Fifty Years of Refugee Studies: From Theory to Policy', *International Migration Review*, Vol. 35 (1): 57–78.

Bloch, A. (1999), Carrying out a survey of refugees: some methodological considerations and guidelines, *Journal of Refugee Studies* 12 (4): 367–383.

Borkert, M. & De Tona, C. (2006), 'Stories of HERMES: a Qualitative Analysis of (Qualitative) Questions of Young Researchers in Migration and Ethnic Studies in Europe', *Forum Qualitative Sozialforschung / Forum: Qualitative Social Research* 7 (3), Art. 9. Available at: http://www.qualitative-research.net/fqs-texte/3-06/06-3-9-e.htm.

Christians, C.G. (2005), 'Ethics and politics in qualitative research', in N.K. Denzin & Y.S. Lincoln (eds.), *Handbook of qualitative research*: 139–164. Third edition. Thousand Oaks CA: Sage Publications.

Cornelius, W. (1982), 'Interviewing undocumented migrants: methodological reflections based on fieldwork in Mexico and the US', *International Migration Review*, Vol. 16 (2): 378–411.

Dench, S., Iphofen, R. & Huws, U. (2004), An EU Code of Ethics for Socio-Economic Research, RESPECT project, funded by the EC IST-Program. http://www.respectproject.org/ethics/412ethics.pdf.

Doornbos, N. (2003), *De papieren asielzoeker. Institutionele communicatie in de asielprocedure*. Nijmegen: Wolf Legal Publishers.

De Lain, M. (2000), *Fieldwork, participation and practice. Ethics and dilemmas in Qualitative research*. London: Sage Publications.

De Tona, C. (2006), 'But What Is Interesting Is the Story of Why and How Migration Happened. Ronit Lentin and Hassan Bousetta in Conversation With Carla De Tona', *Forum Qualitative Sozialforschung / Forum: Qualitative Social Research* [On-line Journal], 7 (3), Art. 13. Available at: http://www.qualitative-research.net/fqs-texte/3-06/06-3-13-e.htm.

Duncan, D.F., J.B. White & T. Nicholson (2003), 'Using internet-based surveys to reach hidden populations: Case of non-abusive illicit drug users', *American Journal of Health Behaviour*, 27(3): 208–218.

Edwards, R. (1990), 'Connecting Method and Epistemology: A White Woman interviewing Black Women', *Women's Studies International Forum*, Vol. 13 (5): 477–490.

Ehlich, K. (1998), 'Vorurteile, Vor-Urteile, Wissenstypen, mentale und diskursive Strukturen', in M. Heinemann (ed.) *Sprachliche und soziale Stereotype*, 11–24. Forum Angewandte Linguistik. Frankfurt: Peter Lang.

Ellis, S. & J. MacGaffey (1996), 'Research on Sub-Saharan Africa's Unrecorded International Trade. Some Methodological and Conceptual Problems', *African Studies Review* 39 (2):19–41.

Engbersen, G., R. Staring, J. van der Leun, J. de Boom, P. van der Heijden & M. Cruijff (2002), *Illegale vreemdelingen in Nederland. Omvang, overkomst, verblijf en uitzetting*. Rotterdam: RISBO Contractresearch BV.

Finckenauer, J.O. & E.J. Waring (1999), *Russian Mafia in America. Immigration, Culture and Crime*, Boston: Northeastern University Press.

Glazer, M. (1982), 'The threat of the stranger: Vulnerability, reciprocity and field-work', in J. Sieber (ed.), *The ethics of social research: Fieldwork, regulation and publication:* 49–70. New York: Springer Verlag.

Global Commission on International Migration (2005), 'Migration in an inter-connected world: New directions for action'. *Report of the Global Commission on International Migration 2005.* Geneva: Global Commission on International Migration.

Gumperz, J.J. & C. Roberts (1991), 'Understanding in intercultural encounters', in J. Blommaert & J. Verschueren (eds.), *The Pragmatics of Intercultural Communication:* 51–90. Amsterdam: John Benjamins.

Grbich, C. (2004), *New approaches in Social Research.* London: Sage Publications.

Harding, S. (1987), 'Is there a Feminist Method?', in: S. Harding (ed.), *Feminism and Methodology.* 1–14, Bloomington: Indiana University Press.

Hartog, J. (2006), 'Beyond "misunderstandings" and "cultural stereotypes"', in K. Bürig & J.D. ten Thije (eds.), *Beyond Misunderstanding.* 175–188. Amsterdam: John Benjamins.

Harrell-Bond, B.E. (1986), *Imposing Aid, Emergency Assistance to Refugees,* Oxford: Oxford University Press.

Harris, S. (1995), 'Pragmatics and Power', *Journal of Pragmatics,* Vol. 23 (2): 117–135.

Heckathorn, D. (1997), 'Respondent-Driven Sampling: A New Approach to the Study of Hidden Populations', *Social Problems,* Vol. 44 (2): 174–199.

Herrera, C.D. (2003), 'A Clash of Methodology and Ethics in "Undercover" Social Science', *Philosophy of the Social Sciences,* Vol. 33 (3): 351–362.

Hobbs, D. (2001), 'Ethnography and the Study of Deviance', in P. Atkinson, A. Coffey, S. Delamont, J. Lofland & L. Lofland (eds.), *Handbook of Ethnography,* 204–219. Sage Publications: London.

Hynes, T. (2003), 'The issue of "trust" or "mistrust" in research with refugees: choices, caveats and considerations for researchers', *UNHCR Working Paper New Issues of refugee studies,* No. 98, November 2003.

Jacobsen, K. & L. Landau (2003), 'Researching refugees: some methodological and ethical considerations', *UNHCR Working Paper: New Issues of Refugee Studies* No. 90, June 2003.

Jandl, M. (2004), 'The Estimation of Illegal Migration in Europe', *Studi Emigrazioni/Migration Studies,* Vol. XLI, No. 153.

Kempadoo, K. & J. Doezema (eds.) (1998), *Global Sex Workers – Rights, Resistance, and Redefinition.* New York/London: Routledge.

Kibreab, G. (2004), 'Pulling the wool over the eyes of the strangers: Refugee Deceit and Trickery in Institutionalized settings', *Journal of Refugee Studies,* Volume 17 (1): 1–26.

Mahler, S.J. & P.R. Pessar (2006), 'Gender Matters: Ethnographers Bring Gender from the Periphery toward the Core of Migration Studies', *International Migration Review,* Vol. 40 (1): 27–63.

Mauthner, M., M. Birch, J. Jessop & T. Miller (2002), *Ethics in Qualitative Research,* London: Sage Publications.

Melrose, M. (2002), 'Labour Pains: Some Considerations on the Difficulties of Researching Juvenile Prostitution', *International Journal of Social Research Methodology,* Vol. 5 (4): 333–351.

Miller, T. & L. Bell (2002), 'Consenting to What? Issues of Access, Gate-Keeping and "Informed" Consent' in: Mauthner, M., M. Birch, J. Jessop & T. Miller (eds.), *Ethics in Qualitative Research*: 53–69, London: Sage Publication.

Minnery, J. & E. Greenhalgh (2007), 'Approaches to Homelessness Policy in Europe, the United States and Australia', *Journal of Social Issues*, Vol. 63 (3): 641–655.

Moore, L.W & M. Miller (1999), 'Initiating Research with Doubly Vulnerable Populations', *Journal of Advanced Nursing*, Vol. 30 (5): 1034–1040.

Phoenix, A. (1994), 'Practising Feminist Research: The Intersection of Gender and "Race" in the Research Process', in Maynard, M. & Purvis, J. (eds), *Researching Women's Lives from a Feminist Perspective*, 49–71. London: Taylor and Francis.

Refugee Studies Centre (2007), 'Ethical Guidelines for Good Research Practice', *Refugee Survey Quarterly*, Vol. 26 (3): 162–172.

Salis Gross, C. (2004). 'Struggling with imaginaries of trauma and trust: the refugee experience in Switzerland', *Culture, Medicine and Psychiatry* Vol. 28: 151–167.

Shuman, A. & C. Bohmer (2004), 'Representing Trauma: Political Asylum Narrative', *Journal of American Folklore* Vol. 117 (466): 394–414.

Smith, G. (2006), 'Hard-to-reach groups don't exist', *Delib* http://www.delib.co.uk/dblog/hard-to-reach-groups-don-t-exist

Smith, L.T (2005), 'On Tricky Ground: Researching the Native in the Age of Uncertainty', in: N.K. Denzin & Y.S Lincoln (eds.), *The Sage Handbook of Qualitative Research*, 3rd edition: 85–108, Thousand Oaks: Sage Publication.

Temple, B., Edwards, R. & Alexander, C. (2006), 'Grasping at Context: Cross Language Qualitative Research as Secondary Qualitative Data Analysis', *Forum Qualitative Sozialforschung / Forum: Qualitative Social Research*, 7 (4), Art. 10. Available at: http://www.qualitative-research.net/fqs-texte/4-06/06-4-10-e.htm.

Trosberg, A. (ed.) (1995), Special Issue: Laying Down the Law – Discourse analysis of legal institutions. *Journal of Pragmatics*, Vol. 23 (1).

Vogel, D. (2002), 'Ausländer ohne Aufenthaltsstatus in Deutschland. Methoden zur Schätzung ihrer Zahl', in E. Minthe (ed.), *Illegale Migration und Schleusungskriminalität*. 65–78. Wiesbaden: Eigenverlag der Kriminologischen Zentralstelle.

Wijers, M. & L. Lap-Chew (1996), *Trafficking in Women, Forced Labour and Slavery-like Practices in Marriage, Domestic Labour and Prostitution*, Bangkok/Utrecht: GAATW.

Wodak, R. (1985), 'The Interaction between Judge and Defendant', in T. van Dijk (ed.), *Handbook of Discourse Analysis*, Vol. IV: *Discourse Analysis in Society*, 181–192. New York: Academic Press.

Wolf, D.L. (1996), 'Situating Feminist Dilemmas in Fieldwork', in D.L. Wolf (ed.), *Feminist Dilemmas in Fieldwork*. 1–55. Colorado: Westview Press.

Zetter, R. (1991), 'Labelling refugees: forming and transforming a bureaucratic identity', *Journal of Refugee Studies*, Vol. 4 (1): 39–62.

PART ONE

Methods and Ethics in Institutional Settings

1

Methodological Issues for the Study of Migrant Incarceration in an Era of Discretion in Law in the Southern USA

ROBERT F. BARSKY

'These are folks who to a large extent came here for the sole reason of earning enough money to send to mama. And they are doing that. And then, on Friday night, they are there with a car. They would never have had a car where they're from. $500 gets you a damned good usable car here, and you couldn't touch one for $500 in Mexico. And they can drive it. License? Maybe. Then some clown shows up drunk one night and sold one of the guys a $200 pistol. There's a really big tradition in Latin America, where if something is happening that is good, then you fire your pistol off. This guy is not a threat to the community. We take the pistol away from him, we tell him why we don't do that, and he goes on. Because the reason they are in jail is the same reason why my Caucasian clients are in jail, – drinking, drugging and being stupid – and just because you come from Mexico and are here to send money home doesn't alleviate any of those three conditions. But what eventually happens to them if arrested depends upon who is working in the jail as to whether, when you are looked up on the computer, that there's a little line on the computer that says 'hold for I.C.E'. When that happens, you are screwed' (an immigration lawyer).

In the current post 9/11 juncture, immigrants and asylum seekers are increasingly spending time in local, state and federal prisons for violation of a host of newly-enacted or newly-enforced laws in a context of heightened security, and this incarceration has as its justification a series of memos, laws, proposed laws and programs which, given their arbitrariness and the high level of discretion that leads to their application, are a kind of legal fiction (see Barsky, 2006a, 2006b). The people who fall into this net, and it's vast, provide a whole new definition of the term 'vulnerable population', an area of study I have pursued through research on asylum seekers, refugees and homeless people since the mid 1990s. The growing number of immigrants in prisons for having violated immigration regulations in the United States, and throughout the Americas, is of concern not only to the huge population of migrants, but to those who are charged with administering and overseeing their detention as well. For this reason, it may be less of a surprise that the Tennessee Department of Corrections (TDOC) has supported the study on intercultural issues relating to incarcerated migrants, for which this chapter provides a methodological basis. The findings presented here will focus upon the situation in the United States and Mexico, however there is growing homogenization with Canadian institutions as well, on account of US pressure and the increasing acceptance on the part of domestic populations in North America that there is a tangible 'security' threat posed by immigrants. As such, this research project applies to all of the NAFTA countries, with implications for any project dealing with similar concerns.

The complex methodological issues arise from a range of factors:

- First, communities of incarcerated individuals are justifiably terrified, and therefore reluctant to speak about their plight even when incarceration authorities allow researchers direct access to them in prisons or incarceration centres.
- Second, few incarceration officials are likely to offer their expertise or access to the incarceration or detention facilities which hold immigrants; in this respect the TDOC (Tennessee Department of Corrections) has been a model in terms of their willingness to cooperate and to smooth relations with the many players to ensure appropriate access for interviews.
- Third, already reluctant interviewees are all the more hesitant in the current juncture when 'the word on the street' is to keep away from officials of all kinds.
- Fourth, the problem of potential or summary incarceration has created heightened tension within immigrant communities who find themselves on the wrong side of new laws, so one way that community officials are encouraging immigrants to survive is to lie as low as possible.
- Fifth, although a range of immigrants are supposed to be held in detention centres, because their 'crime' was to have entered the country illegally, re-entered illegally, or overstayed their visa, the reality is that most land in regular jails, in the first instance and then, once sentenced, in prisons (public and private) – particularly with recent legislation like Operation Streamline (see below). This of course makes it very difficult for researchers who need to get past both the Institutional Review Board guidelines concerning vulnerable populations (next to children prisoners are considered the most vulnerable interview group, and therefore requests are scrutinised with tremendous vigour) and also the ever-stringent policies regulating prisoners.

- Sixth, like any other vulnerable population, incarcerated immigrants are in desperate need of assistance in a number of areas, including legal, medical, psychiatric, personal and intercultural. As such, researchers in this domain find themselves questioned by their interviewees in a way that makes it evident that for many, participation in the research project was contingent on them learning something useful from someone 'official'.
- And finally, the area is so distressing that it's quite challenging to simply do the interviews in an appropriately methodical and professional manner; when the interviewer learns that someone is facing two decades in prison for a combination of a gram of pot, a scuffle in a parking lot, and a return to the US to see his children subsequent to deportation, it's really difficult to remain calm or, heaven forbid, detached.

Methodological issues and discretionary actions

At the end of the day, it's the incredible amount of discretion in this migrant incarceration system that makes this work so difficult, and at times untenable. So on the one hand, I will outline the methodology for a research program appropriate to doing this kind of work; but on the other hand, I will have to pose a preliminary hypothesis about the present concerns in the realm of migrant incarceration in the United States by way of offering a warning to those who would hope for some concrete 'findings' about this group or some rigid approach to this material. Specifically, I will claim that there is in the US a realm of law in which millions of immigrants, legal and illegal, are made so vulnerable by the extraordinary levels of discretion offered to officials at all levels of the system as to put them into a category of almost pure discretion. This means that someone who is illegally living in the US, or even legally living on (say) a visa, is potentially subjected to a whole different realm of legal procedures at all levels, and that the very fact of their being non-citizens makes people more vulnerable to this discretion. It is for this reason that the title of the essay makes reference to 'discretion' alongside of 'methodology', because it is the discretion that makes a formal and predictable methodology inappropriate to the cases of those who violate these vague and unevenly-enforced laws. In these cases, law is no more real than the series of haphazard circumstances that lead to it being invoked; as such, it is neither formalised, nor predictable or linked to the actions which eventually occur.

The instances to which I will refer for a description of this phenomenon arise from a research project on migrant incarceration in the Southern USA, that deals with cases like the thousands of people (potentially tens or even hundreds of thousands of people if more extremist lawmakers manage to push through a 'crack down on illegals' agenda) who are behind bars for a range of immigration violations, including overstaying visas, illegal entry, illegal employment, or illegally re-entering the country subsequent to deportation. These are people, who may have been in the US for a few minutes, or for a few decades, who in some cases have literally grown up, married and worked in this country, and who may even have American wives who have raised with them their American children. They may have worked for large corporations, like Wal-Mart, or they may run their own businesses, paying taxes, employing Americans, and contributing to the community. They can live their whole lives in this country with the knowledge that their US born children will not live in the betwixt-and-between world that they inhabit, which is of course one of the many 'pull factors' that bring people to take the risk of living illegally. Or, and this is the entirely arbitrary or, they can be pulled over for a burnt-out taillight, be flagged by a zealous cop who is unsatisfied with the driving certificate that is issued to people in Tennessee in lieu of a regular license, be taken downtown for being 'illegal', be unable to meet bail fast enough to avoid the zealous paper-pusher in the prison who makes late-night phone calls to Homeland Security or Immigration and Customs Enforcement (ICE.), be sent to a holding institution (jail, prison) to await deportation and, a few days or months later, find themselves 'back' in a country that some of them have not seen for years. If they return subsequent to deportation in order to continue their lives with their families, and if they happen to have any kind of 'felony' charge in their past, including domestic abuse, a drug or gun conviction, or D.U.I. (driving under the influence) they are eligible when stopped again, for whatever reason including a random search, to be sent away for no less than 6 years, and possibly considerably more. Interviewing migrants in this situation is to speak to people who may be willing to place their entire existence into your hands, for me, as a researcher, may represent a tie to the outside world which must be more rational than the Kafkaesque situation in which they have found themselves. Or, on the contrary, I may be another symptom of a discretionary system gone wild, and therefore encounter a stone wall of silence or fear that has grown out of an encounter with a system that is anything other than rational, a system that is, in some sense, fictional except in its consequences.

How can we approach such issues and, for the purposes of this particular contribution, what are the methodological questions that need to be addressed by a researcher interested in dealing with migrant incarceration? The answers to these questions will provide material for this kind of work within and beyond the United States, because even though some of the practices are particular to the US context, there is nevertheless a growing homogeneity of issues across different contexts.

Background of immigration-based incarceration in the US

The context within which immigration-based incarceration is presently occurring has undergone important changes in the last decade, and, in particular, since the adoption of new laws in 1996 (summarised at http://immigration.about.com/gi/dynamic/offsite.htm?site=http://www. shusterman.com/newlawhl.html). After 9/11, many of the new laws were enforced more stringently, and new legislation has been proposed or passed, to the point where no research project in this era could in any serious way rely upon methods or data previously employed. There are truisms which always apply, of course, such as the fact that the more distant one is from the host culture the more difficult it will be to successfully work within the system. This is why people who are refugees, homeless, or even 'foreign' or 'marginal' are going to be subjected to a complex array of 'discrimination' from host country institutions. This is also why Pierre Bourdieu's work on 'language and symbolic power' (Bourdieu, 1991) is always valuable for this kind of work, because he explains the (ill)logic of the discourse marketplace, which buys most discourses from 'foreigners', particularly poor foreigners, at a discount. But the situation has become so severe and widespread in a country like the US, in which millions of people are classified as 'illegal' that it has to defy logic and consistency. This situation has even affected law enforcement officials who now find themselves charged with assessing immigration data, as well as officials involved in incarceration of foreigners in unprecedented numbers, on grounds which can be murky to officials and often incomprehensible to those who find themselves in the system. This study helps to pinpoint the types of difficulties felt by immigrants and asylum seekers who are in the penal system. The findings of this study are being reported and published in order to provide useful information to citizens and officials looking for a comprehensive understanding of the immigrant populations in their midst. Accurate findings will also help alleviate the suffering of immigrants and asylum seekers who are presently trapped in a system they find confusing and ill-reported.

Immigrants in Tennessee

The situation in Tennessee is representative of the national situation, but it is understudied compared to hubs like New York and Miami, and it has certain defining characteristics which deserve in-depth research. The traditionally bi-polar black-white racial system in Tennessee has been destabilised by an unprecedented influx of low-wage immigrants and international refugees over the past decade. According to US Census Bureau,

Tennessee had the sixth fastest rate of immigrant growth (169%) of any state between 1990 and 2000, and the fourth fastest rate of Latino growth (278%). In 2000, the Refugee Services Program of the Nashville and Davidson Country Metropolitan Government estimated that at least one out of every six Nashvillians was born outside the United States. The growth in the refugee populations in Nashville stems from the efforts of the Office of Refugee Resettlement in the US Department of Health and Human Service, and in 2002 Tennessee was among the top five states to receive refugees, a trend that has continued to the present day (see Refugee Resettlement 2007).

Along with this influx comes the problem of incarceration of individuals at an unprecedented rate but, amazingly enough, there are no sources to determine what this means in terms of actual numbers. The reason for this is that this kind of data is not gathered in a systematic way at the time of arrest, and even prison authorities are at a loss to say how many 'foreign-born' people are behind bars; furthermore, because different agencies deal with crime and with immigration violations (the latter being the purview of Homeland Security and I.C.E.), there isn't any central locus to find out such details. So what happens is that an individual with an 'immigration hold' may serve out his or her criminal sentence, and then step out of the prison and into the arms of immigration officials, without the prison officials even realizing that this was going to be the case. Indeed, one reason why this particular research project was considered important by TDOC officials was that it would provide a window into the institutions that they themselves are running, from the perspective of immigration and intercultural relations.

The South has a disproportionate number of immigrant inmates, and states like Tennessee, less historically accustomed to addressing immigrant issues on a large scale than Florida, California or New York because of the relatively recent changes in immigrant demography, are especially affected by recent changes. This is leading to confusion, resentment and fear, leading some law enforcement officials in the South to speak out against what they fear is becoming a dangerous situation. The Nashville Police Chief Ronal Serpas, for example, has been an outspoken figure on the issue of charging law enforcement officials with addressing immigration violations. In an interview with *The Tennessean* (Serpas 2004, cited in a related research report on criminal justice and immigrants, Cox et al. 2004), Serpas stated that 'it's foolish to think that this country's immigration problems are going to be settled on the backs of local police officers'. Serpas is well-placed for such an issue, particularly in light of his experience in the Washington, DC area, where he initiated immigrant awareness programs aimed at addressing intercultural issues relating to Hispanic farm workers who were unaware of local traffic laws. His program, entitled 'El Protector', was an Hispanic education project aimed at aiding foreign workers; his efforts to replicate this program in Nashville shows the importance of a research project which will make available the kind of data appropriate for enacting new programs not only for Hispanics, but for all of the cultural communities with which law enforcement agents must interact regularly.

This project, and the methodology herein described, was proposed in the context of recently-enacted or newly-proposed legislation affecting foreigners, emanating from different Federal, State and local offices. These changes are in themselves a source of great anxiety amongst immigrant and asylum communities, and amongst those charged with enforcing new laws. It's noteworthy that each of these programs has been discussed in the media, but not all have been adopted, or even when adopted they are not consistently adopted from one state, or even one county, to the next. Indeed, the particularities of each proposal is so complex as to require constant monitoring, in part because so many proposals come before state and local legislatures, but so few land up passing, possibly because many proposals are a form of posturing on the part of legislative members trying to prove their 'toughness' to constituents. Furthermore, stated objectives, even of specific police departments, can change from one month to the next; despite Serpas's 2004 claim, for instance, Nashville is now mentioned as a city participating in a crackdown on illegals which usually begins with a routine traffic stop (Howard 2008).

For the purpose of developing a methodology that can somehow account for this set of parameters, notably the psychological effect on immigrants of having potentially applicable laws and regulations, I will provide a brief overview of some of the proposed programs discussed in the media and in legislative assemblies. There have been such an array of programs and initiatives, that an exhaustive list would be a chapter-length work, particularly if it included local, state and federal initiatives; during the week in which this chapter was completed, yet another policy was proposed, 'Operation Streamline', which enforces criminal prosecutions against virtually every person caught illegally crossing stretches of the US-Mexico border. Homeland Security Secretary Michael Chertoff was quoted in testimony to Congress that this new Operation is 'a very good program, and we are working to get it expanded across other parts of the border' because 'it has a great deterrent effect' (Spenser Hsu June 2, 2008). In that same article, T.J. Bonner, President of the National Border Patrol Council, is quoted as saying that 'this strategy pretty much has it backwards. It's going after desperate people who are crossing the border in search of a better way of life, instead of going after employers who are hiring people who have no right to work in this country'. This type of debate is a constant feature of media discussions, usually on the front page (or on leading headlines on such broadcasts as CNN), which creates an atmosphere of fear and uncertainty amongst the population targeted. A short survey provides the sense of how destabilised immigrants must feel as they come to be subjected to ever new, and ever more harsh, measures.

Operation Compliance

Operation Compliance was introduced in Atlanta and Denver as a pilot program to curb the 'chronic' problem of 'absconders' in the immigration system, and could affect up to half a million people in the United States (for details of this program as represented in briefs and in the media, see Chardy 2004, Dougherty 2004, Healey 2004). Because under the pilot program Immigration and Customs Enforcement officers are charged with arresting people who are ordered to leave the country after losing their cases to stay, the system is being overwhelmed by inmates who have been incarcerated for civil rather than criminal reasons. These individuals can now find themselves behind bars while pursuing their rights within the US legal system, even in cases when they came to the US to flee persecution in their own homeland, which leads to a sense of continued persecution and concomitant distress. Previously, foreigners who appealed an immigration decision that went against them were allowed to remain free, and those who lost and agreed to leave the country voluntarily were generally given time to get their affairs in order, usually after posting a bond. Currently, bonds are set at levels completely out of reach for most claimants, and counsel is difficult to procure because most of the immigrants charged have no resources or networks upon which they might rely for assistance. The role of public defenders in this realm is crucial, and the work that they undertake, for very little gain, is generally remarkable.

Authorities charged with overseeing this monumental new responsibility are facing logistical problems relating to costs, training, facilities and manpower. There are only around 20,000 detention beds available nationwide at any given time (Soliz 2006), so to add the civil cases from immigration courts could swamp detention facilities, particularly with indications that some people who land up in the system are condemned to remain therein for long periods of time. This is leading to uneven treatment of immigrants and asylum seekers on the basis of the availability of individuals to adjudicate the claims and prisons to house the growing number of people who are de facto committed to spending time therein.

The CLEAR Act

This research project interviewed immigrants and actors in the system at a time when opponents from local police and governments, victim advocates, and even conservative pundits, were expressing vociferous opposition to legislation that compels state and local police to become federal immigration agents. These bills coerce state and local police into enforcing federal immigration laws by threatening current federal reimbursements if they do not take on these additional duties. The Senate bill goes even further, by imposing new driver's license requirements on state departments of motor vehicles, once again tying federal funding states currently receive to compliance with these new requirements. Police departments like the one in Nashville have worked to build good relations with immigrant communities and encourage immigrants to approach local law enforcement with information on crimes or suspicious activity, and both the CLEAR Act (the Clear Law Enforcement for Criminal Alien Removal (CLEAR) Act, H.R. 2671, introduced by Representative Charles Norwood, R-GA) and HSEA (the Homeland Security Enhancement Act, S. 1906, introduced by Jeff Sessions) are perceived as threats to the relationships they have built with these communities, and will hurt their ability to investigate and solve crimes. Recent compilations of commentary on these issues illuminate these difficulties:

'The act has the potential to shift police priorities so that officers spend their time tracking down immigration violators instead of solving and preventing crimes within their communities. It could also undermine immigrant communities' trust and confidence in law enforcement. Fear of deportation may make immigrants and aliens less likely to report crimes and suspicious activity. Furthermore, foreign nationals may refuse to assist in security investigations because of concerns about the immigration consequences. . . . The proposed legislation is unnecessary. Police already have the authority to arrest aliens who commit crimes, and state and local authorities can help fight terrorism using already established statutory tools'. (James Jay Carafano in The Heritage Foundation, April 21, 2004)

'[I]n the mid-1990s, Congress authorised the attorney general to enter into cooperative agreements with state and local law enforcement officers to allow the latter to serve as immigration officers. Respectful of the principles of federalism and separation of powers between federal and state interests, however, such power was and is strictly voluntary and limited. These precedents, and others, reflect the proper role of the federal government – to enforce federal laws – and the proper responsibility of state and local governments-not to enforce federal laws. The CLEAR Act would throw this important principle out the window in the name of 'fighting the war against illegal immigration'. While this war may be worthwhile, the means of achieving it proposed in the CLEAR Act is not. . . . As a practical matter, forcing local law enforcement to pick up the slack for the federal government's abject failure to use its powers and resources to enforce federal immigration laws, will simply afford the feds another excuse for not doing what they are supposed to have been doing all along. The United States has never before stood for a national police force. Now is not the time to take the first tangible steps in that direction; no matter how appealing the reason'. (Former Georgia Representative Bob Barr (Barr 2004))

Operation Predator

Another example of how these new security-minded powers are being used is 'Operation Predator', (Title 8 C.F.R. 3.19 [i][1][2]), which automatically jails immigrants convicted of sex offences before deporting them. The mass arrests have put hundreds of immigrants, legal and illegal, behind bars for months while they await deportation. A recent report found a federal judge expressing 'serious' doubts about the way the US Department of Homeland Security is using an administrative rule, written to combat terrorism, against sex offenders. The rule is 'wooden', it produces cases that are based on 'quicksand' and it 'may be an abuse' of civil rights, US. District Judge Faith S. Hochberg suggested to the US attorney's office from the bench. The rule has come up in at least six cases in New Jersey and dozens more around the nation, according to attorneys on both sides. The suits charge that programs implemented to guard national security are being used on everyday criminals. 'The regulation was written on Oct. 26, 2001, to enable the government to detain Muslims suspected of being linked to terrorist groups. It allows the DHS to ignore bond decisions or release orders by immigration judges and the Board of Immigration Appeals. It also allows the DHS to keep immigrants in jail at the attorney generals discretion. Although Operation Predator is intended to send home foreign rapists and child molesters, it also has swept up a number of men whose offences were minor, whose convictions were served out years ago and who have lived law-abiding lives since' (Edwards 2004).

Anti-terrorist incarceration techniques

The 'war on terror' has led for calls amongst officials to use stronger tactics in questioning potential terrorists, which places asylum seekers and those experiencing difficulties with their immigration claims in particularly precarious situations. It is also contributing to a significant rise in the population of immigrant and asylum seekers in US prisons, with the host of complex issues it raises for detainees and officials. Much of this is novel for both sides, since recent changes make it such that immigrants who have been incarcerated pending decisions, or asylum seekers who don't have sufficient identification or evidence for their stories, can find themselves incarcerated for indeterminate periods of time while authorities try to simultaneously balance their obligations to uphold security and uphold international law. This situation is rendered more complex by messages sent to local law enforcement and incarceration officials by Washington. In a May 3, 2004 piece entitled 'Fragile Freedoms; Hamdi and Padilla cases will force Supreme Court to find balance between liberty and terror' (*Points of View*), Stuart Taylor Jr. notes that Deputy Solicitor General Paul Clement argued before the Supreme Court for President George W. Bush's claim that 'the military can grab any American suspected of being an 'enemy combatant', anywhere, at any time, and hold him incommunicado for months, years, even for life, with no chance to see a lawyer or tell a court that he is an innocent civilian'. The implications of this message are ominous to detainees, lawmakers and officials since federal review of military determinations of, say, who is an enemy combatant, 'could amount to a rubber stamp, resulting in escalating numbers of Americans thrown into the black hole of incommunicado detention'. Evidence abounds. For instance, on January 27, 2004, the American Civil Liberties Union (ACLU) filed a complaint to a United Nations working group concerning the detention of more than a dozen Arab and Muslim men held by the US without charge following the September 11, 2001 attacks. 'According to the ACLU the indiscriminate arrest of these men and hundreds of others, with no links to terrorism or crime, and their prolonged detention without charge or access to lawyers, violate US commitments under international human rights law'.

The question of which laws are applicable to foreign prisoners regarding participation in research studies is complex, and depends upon the status of the prisoner in this country. In principal, though, US laws apply to these inmates, with various shadings of rights depending upon whether they are deemed asylum seekers, illegal immigrants, green card holders who have committed immigration-violations, or persons 'in transit' through the US. This issue should not have a bearing upon our right to access or their ability to participate in this project.

Demographics and logistics

The enforcement of the abovementioned laws, and the context within which immigrants and asylum seekers are being detained, is leading to a severe rise in the caseloads of immigration courts and the demand for space in correctional facilities, with the concomitant problems associated with both. The situation in Tennessee is serious and not well-documented. Judges Lawrence O. Burman and Charles E. Pazar work at the federal courthouse in Memphis, deciding whether immigrants living in Kentucky, Mississippi, Arkansas and Tennessee get to remain in this country and

ROBERT F. BARSKY

under what conditions, and between 2000 and 2002, their caseload grew from 1,215 to 1,836, a 50% rise, and the trend has continued (for detailed statistics see TRAC 2006). This is at least in part due to the fact that the asylum category has grown since 1995 in Tennessee because the Memphis airport became a hub for Northwest/KLM flights from Amsterdam, making this the first point of entry into the United States. No matter what side of the issue one stands on, the net effect of all these changes and new realities will be to create severe stresses on a strained system, and compound an already obvious need for a better understanding of cultural concerns amongst those involved in the system.

Methodological objectives and proposed approach

This study (completed in April 2008) was originally set up to study incarcerated migrants, and, moreover, individuals who are held for immigration-related concerns, even if this is only one reason for their being held, that is, if there is a criminal concern and also an immigration concern, the person would be part of the study. In order to gather sufficient information prior to undertaking interviews with the prisoners, a large number of community, medical and legal authorities were consulted for interviews. This was undertaken using a snowball approach, whereby each person contacted was asked for a list of other individuals who would be valuable interviewees. The objectives and methodologies for working with the prisoners were then established as follows:

Establishing contact with incarcerated migrants

Incarcerated individuals would be contacted by officials overseeing each of the facilities according to the criteria set out in the description sent to them, that is, persons who are incarcerated for immigration concerns or asylum concerns. Inmates will be excluded if their cases have nothing whatever to do with migration issues. Prison officials themselves will identify incarcerated individuals, and they will make contact with the entire population of eligible interviewees; we will assess the information on those who are willing to participate and choose representative samples of populations to reflect the diversity of concerns (gender, country of origin, status, language).

Participant information would be obtained by the officials involved, that is, Tennessee Corrections, local law enforcement for local jails, and federal officials. Incarceration officials will identify possible participants. We as researchers would not be making contact. We would simply approve suggested subjects offered by the officials, because we are not allowed to undertake solicitation of interviewees in the prisons themselves. The script

36

used to contact inmates is non-coercive, it makes no references to any advantages in doing the study, including parole, and it is emphasised that the participation is voluntary; the Principle Investigator (PI) will be responsible for verifying this. The participant information will be made available by the incarceration officials, and they will make the initial contact.

Specific facilities may have specific rules for recruiting inmates, and therefore it was not possible at the beginning to predict precise methods of contact and follow-up for each institution. We were abode by specific rules set out for recruitment, and work with officials to find an appropriate sampling. The script of the text that was handed out to the inmates reads as follows:

> Robert Barsky, a Professor at Vanderbilt University, is directing a research project about inter-cultural relations amongst inmates held for immigration concerns. Inter-cultural relations refer to elements of interaction between people which are affected by the cultural backgrounds of the individuals in question, notably their race, religion, or country of origin. Inter-cultural relations occur on many levels in interaction, and are manifested through behaviour which reflects awareness of the other person's culture as shown by, for example, fear, respect, prejudice, which specifically relates to culture. Since your case has some immigration elements, you may be eligible to be interviewed for the study. There are no advantages to your being involved in the study, and neither your participation nor your answers will in any way affect any aspect of your case, the conditions of your incarceration, or your treatment. Professor Barsky does hope to assess and improve intercultural relations amongst inmates and between inmates and officials, which means that your participation may help with this general objective. If you are willing to be interviewed for this study, for a period of (roughly) two hours, please indicate below by signing and returning the form to the incarceration official named below. If you choose to participate in the study, you may refuse to answer any question you wish, you may withdraw at any time without consequence, and your identity will be kept strictly confidential in the report of all findings.

When s/he received this signed form, participants would be identified by prison officials who will obtain consent for them to be contacted by me about the study. I have enclosed a letter from Tennessee Corrections allowing the research to go ahead in specific facilities named in the letter.

Language

We anticipated that a large number of incarcerated individuals would be Hispanic, although we were prepared to encounter other languages in relatively large numbers, depending upon the populations involved, include Arabic, Chinese, and Hindi, but we did not restrict ourselves to any language group. As potential interviewees were identified, translation services were contacted within the immigrant communities to act as translators and, where the inmate was quite fluent in English, we conducted interviews in English as well. To ensure consistency and to ensure safety, the PI (the Principal Investigator, Robert Barsky), with the assistance of the researchers on the project, carried out all interviews orally with the different participants in the study (see annex for interview guidelines). The PI was always present, the assistants were present whenever possible, and a translator was present whenever necessary.

The interviews were all conducted by the PI. If the incarceration facility required the presence of an incarceration official, then this person would have been present during the interview as well, but would not be allowed to listen to the proceedings (i.e. if the facility requires that the interview be observed from behind glass, for security purposes; this did not occur in this particular research project). The rationale for using this methodology is that prisoners might reveal something about their criminal case or conviction which was not previously known to the incarceration officials, or s/he might make some kind of accusation about abuse inside of the facility. This could lead to retribution from the guards, or to complicated legal issues relating to the incarceration or the case. Many of the inmates have outstanding issues before the courts, including appeals and pending immigration proceedings, making the interviewing process all the more sensitive.

The role of the PI in this project was to do the interviews with prisoners and undertake the write-up of the report; the role of the assistants is to observe and assist if there are issues (linguistic, contextual) that are raised. The interviews were to be held in accordance with the availability of prisoners and prison officials, subject to their time schedules. The interviews were held in the prison facilities, at times arranged by Tennessee Department of Corrections and the individual facilities. The procedure was to introduce all participants, sign consent forms, conduct oral interviews (recorded), to present the project and ensure that the incarcerated person fully understands the project. Interviews lasted for anywhere from two hours to four hours depending upon the need for translation, the breadth of replies, and so forth. One interview will be held per participant. Follow-ups were deemed to be possible if required based on the need for further information to complete the study.

Ethical issues in the research project

To protect the identity of participants, all information pertaining to the specific identity of the individual will not appear in the published findings or in the reports. No efforts will be made to correlate individuals who may be discussed in the interviews (i.e. if a prisoner speaks of a specific guard). If it may be possible to identify an individual based upon the interview, that part of the interview will not be cited in reports or published findings. Focus in all of the reporting will be upon intercultural and migration issues, so information gathered relating to information about the participant that could be harmful if released will not be included in reports or published materials. For the inmates, proper names will not be used, and the types of information that will be gathered during the interview process will be assessed as regards the entire pool of data gathered, and specific references to utterances by inmates will be restricted to those which pertain to the object of study for the project.

The heavy emphasis upon concealing the identity of the participants reflects the fact that the only risks which could be incurred relate to the release of specific information about the incarcerated interviewees (name, confidential criminal activity), and that information will not appear in the report or published work by the PI or by any member of the workgroup. All interviews with incarcerated persons followed the same criteria for interviews set forth by the officials responsible for their incarceration, in terms of time permitted with the interviewee, the space provided for the interview, the types of recording materials permitted, and so forth.

If accusations of abuse or mistreatment are described by a specific inmate, then the Safety Monitoring Board (SMB), which was set up by the primary researcher and is composed of local experts on incarceration, was to be notified within 24 hours and convened as soon as possible (and definitely within 7 days); this never occurred in this study. Had it occurred, this accusation would then be reported to the Institutional Review Board (IRB) according to the established IRB policy and procedure, as outlined in IRB Policy #III.L. The IRB would be informed of the decision taken by the SMB in the case at hand in relation to the safety/confidentiality of the participant. The SMB contains individuals with training in different aspects of related work, including law, criminal justice, immigrant work, research and ethics. A specific protocol on how to treat this information did not exist since the range of possible information provided and the ideas of what constitutes 'abuse' to individuals is difficult to predict; nevertheless, we did suspect that if specific accusations of abuse were described, prison authorities would be notified so that an investigation could be launched. Pseudo names were assigned to all participants in this project, and all audio and video tapes were marked with the pseudo name instead of real identifiers.

Methodological findings from the current project

With all of this detail as background, it becomes clear that only certain kinds of data, ostensibly qualitative, could be gathered, and under very strong restrictions in terms of citation and publication; so for the current project a number of objectives grew out of the methodology provided herein. First, because of the long lag time between TDOC approval and IRB approval for the interviews with prisoners, it seemed most appropriate to begin interviews with persons familiar with the issue of immigrant incarceration. This was particularly appropriate since it allowed us to establish an understanding of the context within which these prisoners are being arrested and held, and it helped as well in the writing of an appropriate questionnaire to be employed in the prisons.

Second, the difficulty with obtaining meaningful access to incarcerated migrants, and the absence of statistical data concerning the number of immigrants held for immigration violations, the specific effect that immigrant status has upon sentencing, and the impossibility of gaining access to federal facilities, in which refugees and immigrants are held in 'detention', made it such that we would rely more heavily upon the interviews with public defenders, lawyers, interpreters and so forth for details of the incarceration issues, and then use the small number of actual interviews with migrants to confirm some of the findings and to give a voice to this population.

Third, although an original objective was to analyse some intercultural communication issues in the prisons, it became apparent that a larger pool of interviewees would be required to make useful assertions. Because of the small number of incarcerated immigrant interviewees, and because of the extreme vulnerability they experience inside of a very discretion-based and symbolically peculiar penal institution, the most adequate theoretical paradigm is Pierre Bourdieu's work, notably 'Language and Symbolic Power' (Bourdieu 1991).

Fourth, we aimed to determine on the basis of interviews with immigrant inmates what trajectory led them to their present status, how they perceive and describe their current situation, what the situation is between inmates and their families, and what they expect and plan for as regards their future in the US or in their country of origin. Once again, because of the vulnerability of this population, and because they seem on the basis of interviews conducted to be saying what they think we might want to hear, much of the actual data is better amassed with the assistance of lawyers and public defenders. There is also the concern, in any prison, that these 'huis clos' interviews may not be completely private, something that the prisoners themselves fear.

In the end, we hope to provide on the basis of the data accumulated, through interviews and research, some methods of improving relations between inmates, and between inmates and officials, particularly in this period of transition towards Operation Streamline, Homeland Security, Operation Compliance, Operation Predator, the CLEAR Act, and other recent legislation affecting the nature of the inmates and the difficulties they and the officials charged with are likely to face. The results of this research will be shared and discussed with the Tennessee Department of Corrections, the local community, the legal profession, academics, and policy makers, and short articles may also be written for public diffusion via the media to raise public understanding of the issues.

Although the details provided in this chapter apply in quite specific ways to the context of immigrants in the United States, much of the methodology could be applied in any study of immigrant incarceration, if only because of growing homogenization of practices therein. The methodology, as originally described and as modified as per discussions here, have served well as a means of establishing key concerns, and chapters and articles of what will eventually become a full length study are being drafted on this basis. The preliminary conclusions are grim, and, regrettably, with the power of 'security' and 'law and order' discourse, the situation is likely to deteriorate as lawmakers find ways of 'putting people away' without, in fact, considering the effects, long and short term, of these practices. A lot of angry people are being born in prisons and internment centres throughout the world, and if 'terror' is indeed spread by the alienated, the disenfranchised, and those with nothing more to lose, not much good can come of current practices.

Acknowledgement

I would like to thank the Centre for the Americas, Vanderbilt University, for supporting this project as an 'incubator' and then as a 'workgroup'. Discussions with members of this workgroup were of great value in producing the substance of this work, and Fabrice Picon and Alham Usman, student assistants to the group, were invaluable throughout the project. I am also grateful for the regular input of the Institutional Review Board, particularly for issues of methodology, and for the support of the Tennessee Department of Corrections. And finally, thanks to Marsha Tardy, for everything.

Bibliography

Barr, B. (2004), *Outside View: Clear as mud*, United Press International, on-line at: http://www.immigrationforum.org/DesktopDefault.aspx?tabid=587

Barsky, R.F. (2006a), 'From Discretion to Fictional Law', *SubStance* issue 109 Vol. 35 (1): 116–146.

Barsky, R.F (2006b), 'Activist Translation in an Era of Fictional Law', *Translation and Social Activism, TTR* XVIII. Vol 2 (2007): 17–48.

Bourdieu, P. (1991), *Language and Symbolic Power*, Cambridge, MA: Harvard University Press.

Carafano, J. J. (2004), *The Heritage Foundation* (April 21, 2004). All Heritage reports are available on-line at: http://www.heritage.org/Research/HomelandSecurity/wm941.cfm.
Chardy, A. (2004), *New program raises stakes for foreign nationals*, on-line at: http://www.durrani.com/newsite/news_items/nactive_disp.asp?ID=666.
Cox McKenna, K. Pride, & M. Wright (2004), *Tennessee Immigrants and Criminal Justice*, available at: http://www.law.utk.edu/Library/teachinglearning/ permanent/LU/lupstory1.html.
Dougherty, J. E. (2004), *Pilot Program Jails Immigration Case Losers*, NewsMax, online at: http://archive.newsmax.com/archives/articles/2004/4/28/90906.html.
Healey, S. A. (2004), 'The Trend Toward the Criminalization and Detention of Asylum Seekers' in *Human Rights Brief*, Volume 12 Issue 1, on-line at: http://www.wcl.american.edu/hrbrief/12/1healey.cfm
Edwards, J. (2004), 'Jailing of Immigrants Triggers Litigation: Three on federal bench frown at government's use of Sept. 11 rule against everyday criminals'. *New Jersey Law Journal*, on-line at: http://www.law.com/jsp/article.jsp?id=1074259242113
Howard, K. (2008), 'Metro traffic stops lead to most deportations: Sheriff's immigration crackdown catches more minor offenders than violent criminals' in *Americans for Legal Immigration*, on-line at http://www.alipac.us/modules.php?name=News&file=article&sid=3138.
Hsu, S. (2008), 'New Policy May Keep Out Border Infiltrators' in *The Tennessean* A1. June 2, 2008.
Refugee Resettlement Watch (2007), volume 1.1, on-line at: http://refugeeresettlementwatch.wordpress.com/refugee-resettlement-fact-sheets
Serpas, R. (2004), 'Immigration enforcement not role for police, Serpas says' in *The Tennessean*, A1. April 5, 2004.
Soliz, R. (2006), 'US Marshals Announce Scaleback of Superjail Proposal', in *CAJE Project*, on-line at: http://cajeproject.org/blog/?cat=2.
Taylor, S. (2004), 'Fragile Freedoms; Hamdi and Padilla cases will force Supreme Court to find balance between liberty and terror' in *Points of View*. May 3, 2004.
TRAC 2006, on-line at: http://trac.syr.edu/immigration/reports/ 183/include/1_judgelist.html.

Annex: Interview guidelines

Sample Questionnaire for inmates

1. Identification
   - Sex.
   - Year and place of birth.
   - Ethnic origin and Religion.
   - Languages spoken/written.
   - Marital Status.
   - Spouse's ethnic origin.
   - Children, if any: number.

Sex   Place of birth   Year of birth

- Are the children in the USA? Age and education of children at the time of arrival in US.
- Relatives (or spouse) outside of the country of origin.
- Relatives in the USA? When did they arrive?
- Did you have on-going relations with relatives in Tennessee or the USA prior to departure from your country of origin? What form? [phone, letter, . . .].
- When was the last time you communicated with family members? With whom?
- Do you have any contact with people other than inmates and family members? Who?
- Overall, who knows that you have been incarcerated?
- Have you lived in other countries? When? Where? Reasons for moving there.
- What legal status did you request in these countries, and what legal status did you obtain?
- When did you arrive in the USA? From where? What was your experience at the border?
- What is your current immigration status?
- Have you travelled back to your country of origin since arriving in the USA? When?
- Had you ever visited the USA before coming here? When and why?
- Did you know anything about the USA's immigration laws prior to your coming here?
- What kind of job did you think you would obtain in the USA?
- What city did you think you would live in?
- What kind of neighbourhood did you think you would live in?
- If you don't speak English, how did you expect to learn the language?
- What was your image of the USA?
- How have you changed since coming to the USA?
- How have you changed since being incarcerated?
- How do you feel overall?
- How do you envision your future? Do you have a future in America? In Nashville?
- Have you been in court? When?
- Did you have a lawyer? Or some other representative?
- If YES: Were you able to effectively communicate with your lawyer?
- Had you known other people who have been arrested in the US before being incarcerated?
- Did you know that you could be arrested for whatever you were doing that led to your arrest?
- Did you feel that the crime for which you are incarcerated matches the punishment you have received?
- How long have you been in this prison? How much longer will you stay?
- Have you filed an appeal?
- What is a typical day like for you here?
- Do you have anyone you can express your questions and concerns to here?

- Are you a religious or spiritual person?
- How do you practice your religion/spirituality?
- Have you ever had difficulties practicing your religion/spirituality?
- Do you know where this incarceration facility is located?
- Have you moved since being incarcerated, from one facility to another? Why? When?
- Had you been incarcerated before? In the USA? In your country of origin?
- What are your relations like with prison officials?
- Do you have difficulties communicating with officials at this institution?
- Are there other prisoners from your country or cultural background in this prison?
- Do you have good relations with other prisoners from your culture? Other cultures?
- What are your obligations as a prisoner here?
- What do you expect out of the officials working in this facility?
- Have you changed your sense of cultural identity since being incarcerated?
- What concrete measures could be taken to improve communication in the prison?
- What other measures would make this prison better?
- Do you have any training programs? Do you have access to television stations, books, magazines or radio in your language?
- If you have been incarcerated before, compare it with this experience you're having now.
- If you could say something to a high-ranking government official, what would it be? [warden, governor, president, . . .] What would you say to police officials if you could? Judges? The general public?

Sample Questionnaire for lawyers, public defenders and legal experts

We are going to ask you some questions concerning your own impressions of the migrant incarceration issue, and also your sense of how migrants themselves perceive their own situations. We'll also be asking you about your own interactions with those clients of yours who are in the incarceration system. Our objective is to study all facets of this issue by interviewing a host of people who have knowledge of the incarceration issue as it pertains to migrants, and then to interview the migrants themselves in the prison facilities to which we have been given access. Your identity will be concealed, so anything you say for this interview will, if mentioned in the report, be referred to in terms of your experience, and as someone with intimate knowledge of the system.

1. Identification/personal history
- Gender
- Year of birth

- Place of birth (town, province, state)
- Ethnic origin
- Do you practice any religion?
- What religion were/are their parents or family 'back home'?
- Do you practice such a tradition or do you follow a different faith tradition?
- Education [degrees, domain]

2. Career trajectory

We're interested in the professional trajectory that led you to work with immigrants.

- When did you begin to work with immigrants and asylum seekers?

Migrant related work   Period   Location

a.

b.

c.

- Why did you choose this area of work?
- Before your current job, did you have contact with persons incarcerated for immigration or asylum issues? Where? What form of contact? [telephone, letter . . .]
- Have you ever worked in the prison system? If so, in what capacity?
- What kind of legal experience do you have?
- What kind of training do you have in immigration or refugee law? [law school, clinics, after law school]
- Have you been in court to act on behalf of incarcerated immigrants? Explain.
- Have you ever helped an inmate before the INS or Homeland Security?
- Do you work with other groups which are involved from a judicial standpoint in immigration issues or the legal process? Which ones? For what reason?

3. Cultural knowledge/experience

- Languages spoken
- Languages written
- Have you lived in other countries? [years, duration, location]
- Have you ever had contact with immigrants in places outside of your employment? When, where, which communities, what type of contact?
- Have you ever had any kind of cultural training [cultural sensitivity, intercultural communication]. When and where?
- Has working with immigrants affected your sense of your own culture? If so, how?

4. Current experience with incarcerated persons

I will now ask you about your own current experience with migrants who have been arrested or incarcerated.

- What is your current work with immigrants?

- Do you specialize in working with particular legal categories of immigrants?
- What is the legal status of the immigrants with whom you actually work (undocumented, guest workers, asylum seekers etc)? what percentage of each?
- What country do your clients come from [break down according to area]. What percentage of your clients are female? Where are they from?
- Do you have communication or contact with incarcerated persons? What type? [prison visits, phone calls, letters]
- Do you have a sense of what kinds of offences immigrants are generally arrested for?
- Does the type of offence vary by cultural group?
- What offences are committed by those immigrants with whom you yourself have contact?
- Has the type of offence for which people are arrested changed in the past five years? Please explain.
- In your experience, are immigrants targeted for arrest? Under what conditions? Are some immigrants targeted more than others? Please explain.
- What is the process that immigrants follow upon being arrested that leads them into the prison system?
- Do you have dealings with immigrants who are arrested for some non-immigration related crime and then find themselves charged with immigration related offences? [Please explain].
- Do you have dealings with people who are incarcerated only for immigration reasons? Where are they incarcerated, and what is the process that led to their being incarcerated?
- In your experience, are immigrants aware that crimes such as DUI or domestic abuse can lead to incarceration for immigration violations?
- In terms of legal issues [rights, appeals, corrections, remedies] how has treatment of immigrants changed since September 11, in your experience? How do you feel about these changes?
- How have incarceration procedures changed since September 11, in your experience? How do you feel about these changes?

5. Interactions between lawyer and client
- How do you think immigrants of different cultural backgrounds understand your role as a lawyer in this process?
- In your opinion, do claimants have more trust in lawyers from their own culture?
- Have you ever had difficulties communicating with immigrant clients? Explain.
- Are some groups more difficult to communicate with than others?
- What are some of the types of cultural misunderstandings that you've experienced?
- Do you use a translator when communicating with immigrant clients?

- If you use translators, how does this affect your work with clients? [hurt, help]
- Is the lawyer-client relationship affected by using translators? In what sense?
- To whom do you speak when you have questions relating to the culture of your clients?
- Would it be useful for you to have a cultural mediator of some sort to assist you with intercultural issues? Explain.
- Have intercultural problems ever affected your ability to practice the law with clients?
- Have you ever felt that a client did not trust you?
- Have you ever felt distrust towards a client? (being lied to, etc.) Explain. Are the issues cultural?
- Have you ever had any specific gender issues when dealing with clients from specific cultures?

6. Perceptions of incarcerated persons experience

We will now ask you, from your perspective, some questions about how your clients experience the incarceration process.

- How would you describe incarcerated immigrants knowledge of the law as it pertains to their case? [please distinguish between the knowledge they have of non-immigration related crimes versus immigration-related crimes] Does it differ from other incarcerated persons?
- What reaction do migrants have to being incarcerated for reasons pertaining to migration? [emotional reactions, strategic reactions, etc.] How does this compare to reactions about being incarcerated for non-migration crimes?
- What do you see to be the expectations of these incarcerated immigrants? [please distinguish between different legal categories, notably asylum seekers, illegal immigrants, etc.]
- Do incarcerated immigrants think they will be deported?
- Do incarcerated immigrants think they will be imprisoned for a long time?
- Do incarcerated immigrants expect to have legal representation?
- Do incarcerated immigrants expect to receive assistance from officials from their country of origin? Should they, in your opinion?
- Do incarcerated immigrants seek assistance from their families? From their communities? In what way?
- What type of assistance do you seek for immigrants from their countries of origin, if any?
- Do you have any contact with inmates family members? Who? When?
- What are inmates obligations as prisoners here, what do they have to do other than just await the passage of time?
- Do incarcerated immigrants have access to resources in the prisons that can help them with their cases? What kind?
- Are there any musical activities allowed within the prison?

- If so, what are those activities? What in your opinion do they add to the culture of incarceration? Are the musical activities from 'home', or are they locally learned?

7. Cultural concerns amongst incarcerated migrants
- Do incarcerated immigrants frequently complain about cultural concerns in the prisons?
- How do incarcerated immigrants specifically act out their faith/religion when incarcerated?
- Do incarcerated immigrants have any difficulties praying?
- Do incarcerated immigrants have any difficulties practicing their religion? What types of difficulties do they have?
- Are incarcerated immigrants provided with appropriate diets given their cultures? And appropriate clothing?
- Do incarcerated immigrants complain about dietary issues? Clothing concerns?
- Do incarcerated immigrants have anyone with whom they can express your questions and concerns about cultural issues, or other matters, in prisons?
- What kinds of communication issues come up in the prisons? [between prisoner and guards, between prisoners, . . .]
- Do inmates tend to have good relations with other prisoners from their culture?
- Do inmates tend to hang out with prisoners from their own culture?
- Are there any particular issues (antagonisms, bonding) between inmates from different cultures? Between immigrants and American inmates?
- What concrete measures could be taken to improve communication in the prison?
- Do prisons have intercultural training programs? Should they?
- Do you work with a prisoner representative who helps you with official issues? What kind?
- Do you feel that broader cultural discourses, from the government, the media or elsewhere, affect your work with incarcerated migrants? In what way?
- What measures would make the prison system better for those incarcerated for migration reasons?
- What do you think about the incarceration of immigrants for immigration offences?
- If you could say something to a high-ranking government official about intercultural communications between migrants and officials, including yourself, what would it be? [warden, governor, president, ...]
- Is there anything you'd like to add?

2

Multi-Perspective Research on Foreigners in Prisons in Switzerland

CHRISTIN ACHERMANN

Telling someone about my research on foreigners in prisons usually provokes spontaneous emotional reactions: some people express the fears they would have of talking to criminals (mostly thought of being male) and admire the supposed courage of facing such a challenge. Others wonder whether they would stand talking to these poor persons incarcerated far from home – in these cases the inmates are mainly thought of being women. And some people are suspicious of the aim of the study because they suppose it must include showing sympathy towards offenders or, even worse, that the research aims at excusing foreign offenders and presenting them as victims. Many people however are simply fascinated and curious to know what a prison in Switzerland looks like, how inmates live, how they are treated by staff, how it feels to talk to them and to work in this very specific and mostly hidden context to outsiders. Before entering a prison for the first time, it was a mixture of these questions and attitudes I had in my mind, too. And all along the process of data gathering, transcribing and analysing these different aspects of curiosity, of positive and negative emotions, the ambiguity towards inmates and staff were present, although in steady evolution and change. However, I got accustomed to working behind bars and security fences quite quickly. Meanwhile, my colleagues and friends started to get used to my new working area as well and even began to like telling others with a smile that I was in prison when out of office.

No doubt, prisons are special places, with their own logic and rules and full of ambiguity – for inmates, staff and also researchers. And it is obvious that a series of methodological and ethical questions related to security, confidentiality, independence, trust and power have to be dealt with. This chapter aims at giving insight into a research project on foreign national inmates in two closed penitentiaries in Switzerland focusing on methodological aspects and their ethical and personal implications for the researchers. The focus on this special group of foreign inmates implied particular ethical and methodological concerns as these people often are socially isolated and in precarious situations as far as their legal and/or socio-economic position is concerned. In order to grasp and understand the situation of foreign inmates and what their high share in Swiss prisons implies for the penal institutions and the responsible administrative services the project followed a multi-perspective approach. This way, all groups of actors involved (foreign inmates, prison staff, and administrative staff) were given the opportunity to express their point of view. Thus, a deep understanding of the diverse processes being under way was striven for. However, this approach entailed at the same time difficulties and caused dilemmas the research team had to deal with in the course of its work.

In the following, the multi-perspective approach to organisational settings in the migration context will be presented and its advantages and disadvantages will be reflected on. Second, the chapter will focus on the specific context of doing research in penal institutions in general and in particular on foreign national inmates, highlighting methodological aspects that turned out to be of particular use and pointing to ethical challenges.

Foreigners in closed prisons: background information

Before pointing out the methodological and ethical questions in this specific study the context in which this study took place will be sketched. Foreign national prisoners are increasing in numbers in most European countries (Tomaševski 1994, Van Kalmthout et al. 2007a, 2007b). With a share of 69% in 2006, Switzerland is among those European countries with the highest rates of foreign national inmates.[1] Despite an intense public debate on this high share and on so-called 'foreigners' criminality', very little is known about the situation and background of foreign inmates or about the consequences of this trend for Swiss prisons.[2] This lack of reliable data led to a research project dealing with the situation of foreign inmates in two – in Swiss terminology – 'closed prisons'.[3] The main interest of this study was to know more about the imprisoned foreigners (who they are and how they experience doing time in Switzerland), to understand the reasons for this high share and to reflect on how staff of the penal institutions is dealing with the changing set up of prisons and how this affects the practice of the prison department and in particular the migration service.

'Closed prisons' are institutions originally intended for recidivist offenders with a medium to high level of security. Since by law foreign national convicts can be expelled after release because they are considered to be 'unwanted',[4] the risk of escape is taken for granted and generally, these inmates are placed in closed prisons with highly restricted opportunities to leave. This leads to a clear overrepresentation of 70–80% foreign national inmates in this type of custody (Bundesamt für Statistik 2007).

For the same reason, also remand prisons show very high rates of foreign national inmates. On the contrary, when it comes to so-called 'open' prisons or alternative sanctions as Electronic Monitoring, Swiss prisoners are clearly in the majority.[5]

After serving their time, foreign nationals can be deported from Switzerland on the basis of their legal status as 'non-national' and depending on the seriousness of their offence. This means that when being sentenced for a criminal act, citizenship makes a difference. Hence, foreign national inmates find themselves in a situation of 'double exclusion' by both the penal law and by the foreign nationals act. This means that after being excluded temporarily from participating in everyday social life by incarceration, foreign national convicts run the risk of further being expelled from the Swiss territory and being forced to return to their country of origin. In contrast, Swiss citizens cannot be expelled from their home country since they are enjoying an unrestricted right of abode which is exclusively granted to them. Hence, the consequences of a criminal offence differ according to the legal status of the convict. Unlike the recently much debated topic of detention and deportation of undocumented migrants or rejected asylum seekers because of their 'illegal' stay, this study deals with foreign nationals who have been sentenced by a penal court in Switzerland and who have served their time in prison. Some of them are indeed undocumented migrants, but all of them – according to the court – have committed a crime. In some cases, 'illegal' stay was in fact one of several reasons for the sentence, but it was hardly ever the main reason for being incarcerated in one of the closed prisons. Furthermore, the penitentiaries talked about here needs to be distinguished from detention centres for irregular migrants. Not only are the latter exclusively intended for foreign nationals, they are also based on different legal grounds than penitentiaries (administrative foreign nationals act vs. penal code).

This study is interdisciplinary in the sense that it used an ethnographic approach in combination with a historical focus in two Swiss prisons and in the respective administrative units, i.e. the migration service and the prison department. The prisons of Hindelbank with a capacity for 107 female inmates and Thorberg with one for 165 male inmates are both located in the Canton of Bern. In 2004, the rate of foreign inmates was at 89% for men in Thorberg and at 50% for women in Hindelbank. Apart from the common characteristics of potential double exclusion the group of foreign prisoners in the Swiss penal system shows a great deal of diversity with regard to nationality, religion, socio-economic background, offences, etc. The presence of large groups of foreign inmates is not a new phenomenon in Swiss penitentiaries. In Thorberg Swiss inmates became a minority by the mid-1980s while in Hindelbank this happened ten years later. Despite many years of experience in dealing with an increasingly more heterogeneous group of inmates, the shifting composition of these groups remains a major challenge for the prisons. Due to the fact that such changes as regards to characteristics and number of inmates can hardly be foretold, the management is left with a reduced room for manoeuvre in the anticipation of appropriate action. Diversity management as a basic strategy in coping with this situation is not widely adopted yet.[6] One goal of the study was to understand the complex process of interaction between the prison service and the migration office in decision-making with regard to the expulsion of an inmate after release. For many of the inmates who later will be deported, this decision becomes final only towards the end of their stay in prison since a majority of foreign prisoners must leave Switzerland after release. As a result rehabilitation efforts during their stay tend to become neglected.[7]

Methodological approach:
Multi-perspective research design

Ethical questions are omnipresent in qualitative research based on face-to-face interactions. This is even truer when studying migrants and their lives in a foreign country. One reason for this is the personal nature of interviewing, observing and participating in their lives. Much more than in rather anonymous and standardised interactions with interviewees or when working with administratively gathered data bases, in qualitative interviewing or participant observation researchers get involved as 'full persons' into interactions and a personal relationship to the researched persons is built up, albeit mostly only a temporary one. In this situation, a lot of questions arise that turn around topics like professionalism, distance and involvement, obligations towards the research partners etc. Working with migrants in precarious situations enhances the complexity of these aspects as very often there is considerable status difference between the researcher and the researched as far as legal status/ citizenship, socio-economic position and often also education are concerned. Choosing an appropriate methodological approach can contribute to reducing ethical tensions. A multi-perspective research design that aims at understanding a given phenomenon and the intertwining agency of a variety of actors can be one possibility. In the following such an approach will be presented and its potentials and difficulties discussed thereby drawing on experiences from two concrete studies. The first is an application for a research project on the naturalisation process in a Swiss city (Achermann & Gass 2003) and the second the already mentioned study on foreign national inmates in closed prisons where a similar design was used, however enlarged considerably in scope and complexity.

The idea of capturing a given social phenomenon in its broadest sense by taking into consideration the intertwining and mutually influencing structural conditions and the agency of individuals in their varying appearances is typical for anthropological research. In classical anthropological studies a holistic view was mainly achieved by participant observation which was ideally done while spending a one year cycle in a community (e.g. Malinowski 1972). For migration research in organisational settings however, other methodological tools for attaining a broad, deep and multi-faceted view seem to be more practicable and adequate. Through triangulation of a variety of perspectives and of different kinds of data such a comprehensive understanding can be approached. Its advantages are twofold: On the one hand, the complexity of a given phenomenon is grasped by giving a voice and listening to all the (groups of) actors implied in a given setting. On the other hand, combining multiple types of data is thought to enhance understanding.

Such an approach can be situated in the Weberian tradition of sociology that is concerned 'with the interpretive understanding of social action and thereby with a causal explanation of its course and consequences' (Weber 1968). Liebling (1999: 163) points to the fact that 'to understand and promote understanding' is a task of researchers and part of their work and that by only combining a variety of data, including emotions, 'a deep kind of knowledge that feels like understanding' can be achieved. However, such a multi-perspective approach dealing with diverse data should not be understood as a means for finding 'the truth' or 'the reality'. Instead of giving simple answers researchers will rather be confronted with the complexity of social life. Of course, different perspectives and data can and are thought to complement each other and thereby foster a comprehensive understanding of certain processes. Nevertheless, the outcome of triangulation will often not be one clear picture of composed parts of a puzzle that would correspond to 'the objective truth'. Researchers will rather face a multidimensional picture whose colours, shadings and clear, blur or black parts change according to the perspective from which it is presented or looked at. Far from striving for objective and absolute results, multi-perspective research rather aims at making visible, transparent and understandable the complex, manifold and sometimes contradictory processes of social life.

Outline of a multi-perspective research design

In the study on foreigners in two closed prisons in the Swiss Canton of Bern we opted for this methodological approach because the project aimed at a balanced and deep understanding of a complex subject that had not been investigated yet. It seemed important not to limit to partial views in order to overcome the numerous biases in the field of prisons and criminal foreigners. To illustrate how exactly such a multi-perspective research could look like, the procedure of data collection will be presented on this example. In order to distinguish the different perspectives and types of data the description follows an analytical distinction between different research phases. However, in practice these stages always overlap and intermingle (cf. Table 3.1 for an overview).

Variety of perspectives

Two groups of actors take centre stage: the foreign inmates on the one side and members of staff on the other side.[8] Together they constitute the members of the two penal institutions and their actions and interactions structure life within. Although sharing certain characteristics because of their common structural position, it has to be stressed that both groups are not homogenous entities but consist of very different 'elements', i.e. a great variety of inmates (as far as age, gender, origin, offence, legal status, family situation is concerned) as well as, to a slighter extent, different members of staff of different sections of the penitentiary (e.g. management, guardians, social workers, workshops, administration, health service) with varying individual backgrounds, too. The responsible administrative offices, i.e. the migration service (the cantonal immigration agency in charge of decision-making regarding the deportation of foreign national offenders upon their release from prison) and the prison department (the enforcement agency responsible for incarcerating all persons sentenced by the cantonal courts) and their members represent actors of secondary importance. They are not directly part of life in the penitentiaries, but their decisions on conditions of the enforcement of sentences (e.g. right to leaves, change to more open institutions, and release on parole) or on expulsion are of great importance to the present and future of the inmates and influence therefore their life as well as staff's work in the penitentiary. Another structuring source is the relevant *law* which determines the conditions of acting of all the actors mentioned and is situated within a given socio-political context. Members of civil society, as for instance experts, members of NGOs or researchers, are considered to be part of that context.

Variety of data

How to capture this variety of perspectives and dimensions in the data collection is a challenge. In order to understand the legal context, we studied the various kinds of legal texts and regulations. Information on the broader socio-political context was collected from scientific literature, newspaper articles, and expert interviews. The latter also provided us with an external view on the topic of foreigners in Swiss prisons and some of them gave us important information on doing research within penal institutions.

Information on the various groups of actors was collected through semi-structured interviews. We first conducted interviews with a total of 60 foreign national inmates (27 female, 33 male).[9] The interviews lasted for about two hours each and were done in ten different languages.[10] The interviews took place in a visitors' room and no member of prison staff was present. Interviews were done with two researchers (one female, one male) present: one actually conducting the interview, the other assisting by taking notes in order to have a short protocol of the talk, controlling technical equipment, and checking completeness of the questions discussed as well as time. Interviews focused on the personal experience of prison stay, on contacts to the outside world, on preparation for release and plans for the future. The offence they were convicted for was not part of the interview questions. Interviews with staff (35) were of the same type as with inmates: they followed a semi-structured guideline, were done individually, recorded and lasted up to a maximum of 2 hours. Every section of the penitentiary was represented; out of the groups with close contact to the inmates (guardians, workshops, and social service) several collaborators were interviewed. They were asked about their work in general and about what was specific to working with foreign national inmates.

A third group of interviews was done with staff of the two administrative units (12).[11] In these interviews we were mainly interested in getting to know their tasks and competence and in understanding the decision making processes they were responsible for, what criteria they applied and in specific questions related to foreign national offenders.

Another important source of information was samples of inmates' files in the penitentiaries (686) as well as at migration service (299)[12] from the past twenty years. Prison files were chosen randomly. They contain some information on an inmate's offence and judgement and mainly document what has happened since the person has entered the institution (e.g. letters to the management, decisions concerning workplace, education, preparations for release, visits, and leaves). Files at migration service were chosen in order to complement the selected prison files. They mainly inform about immigration topics, among them the decision making process on future deportation of foreign offenders. In general, files provide on the one hand information on inmates, on the other hand they contain specific examples of the decisions and the way administrations and penal institutions work and interact with inmates and how this might have changed over time. The randomly sampled files also provide quantitative data on prison population and their evolution, information on measures taken (e.g. deportation) or rights granted to them (e.g. leaves). Such information can be used for descriptive statistics and give a broad view of the past and present population and their characteristics. Besides, this information helps to contextualise the cases of the interviewed inmates. As regards to information on individual inmates, we additionally included files of all the inmates who had been interviewed in order to get background information on their prison stay and their biography, including their 'criminal career'. All data on files were collected in a database with a number of pre-determined variables and several 'open' fields for diverse, mainly qualitative data. I will come back to the ethical implications of this method later on.

The analysis of the annual reports (1960–2003) of the penitentiaries added further elements to the historical perspective. Based on this, we were able to reconstruct at what stage foreigners became an important topic in the penal institutions, what staff of different prison sections (e.g. medical doctor, pastor, social assistants) wrote about them, or what other topics or problems were relevant in a given year. Besides this contextual information the reports contain detailed statistics on the prison population which broaden and complement the information taken out of the files. Raw quantitative data on all the foreign inmates who were in the two penitentiaries since 1983 was provided by the Swiss Federal Office of Statistics. This information on offence, demography, sentences and stay in the institutions served on the one hand for the sampling for file analysis in the penitentiaries. On the other hand they provide complete overviews of the population that can complement the information taken out of the annual reports.

Table 3.1 Perspectives and types of data

Perspective	Type of data
Legal context/ juridical view[1]	Legal texts (international, national, cantonal), internal regulations of penitentiaries
Socio-political context	Scientific literature, newspapers, expert interviews
Male and female foreign national inmates	Interviews; files in penitentiaries and at migration service; observation
Members of staff representing all the sections of the penal institutions	Interviews; files; observation
Members of staff of the two responsible administrative services	Interviews; files
Diachronical view	Files; annual reports; statistical data

In order not just to work with 'second-hand information' from written or oral sources, we did small scale participant observation in the penitentiaries at different occasions. These were possibilities to gather ethnographic data on interactions as well as the architecture and arrangement of the penitentiaries, but also to talk informally to inmates and staff.

At the very beginning of the study we spent five entire days in the female prison. There, we passed the day in the same way as the inmates: working, eating and leisure time in the evening. However, when the inmates were locked in their cells, we stood on the guardian's side of the door and left the penitentiary soon after to come back the next morning. This way, we got to know all of the sections where inmates live together as well as the different workplaces. In the male prison such an extensive stay was not possible, mainly due to security reasons. There, we mainly observed a day with a guardian who showed us around from the moment of unlocking the cells at 6:45 until closing them again at 21:30. Additional, but often only short occasions for observations were given whenever we stayed at the penitentiaries for interviews or file analysis. All of these experiences and observations were recorded in field notes.

Potentials of a multi-perspective research

The main advantages of such a comprehensive research design can be summarised as follows: first of all, it enables a deep as well as broad insight and understanding by taking into account different aspects and variables of a given process. It is therefore especially useful for understanding complex settings with a variety of implicated groups of actors and inter-twining processes. The comprehensive understanding is striven for on the one hand by approaching a phenomenon from different perspectives that enables a triangulation of viewpoints. On the other hand, a differentiated, detailed and well-founded view is acquired by a combination of data: comparing and juxtaposing for instance interviews – that inform the researcher about what people think and how they talk about something, how they interpret phenomena, how they remember things that have happened etc. – to other data enables a much deeper understanding of the ongoing processes and of why people act in a given way. For instance, yearly reports, administrative files, statistics, laws and regulations additionally inform about the structuring conditions that are thought of as being enabling and constraining at the same time (see Giddens 1984). And observations of what people actually *do* and how they behave as well as the researchers' experiences and reflections again provide other dimensions.

Besides these epistemological advantages, such an approach can be considered to be positive from an ethical standpoint: Talking and listening to all the important actors and giving them the opportunity to express their own views is one possibility of taking serious and dealing in a respectful way with persons (migrants, staff and administration) under study. For instance, in a context where stereotypes about 'bad inmates' and 'good staff' are as common as their opposite the 'poor inmates' and 'bad staff', such a balanced methodology can be of great value. But also in (migration) research with people in precarious situations it is essential to aim for a balanced picture because typically, marginalised persons rarely express their views towards outsiders and others ('experts') often only have selective knowledge about their lives.

Additionally, a multi-perspective approach is of special interest for legal anthropology or sociology interested in the structural juridical conditions and their enactment by individual actors (i.e. members of administrations and prisons). The approach of taking into account not only written law and jurisdiction, but also the practice and multiple perspectives of the groups of actors involved, aims for capturing these social phenomena in the most comprehensive way possible. Such an approach is of particular use in contexts that are characterised by large scopes of discretion, i.e. where legal texts do not regulate clearly how to interpret and/or enact what they lay down. As a consequence, the individual members of administration who are responsible for instance for enforcement of sentences, deportation procedures or naturalisation have to shape and interpret the vague legal texts on their own, often based on their own subjective interpretations. Applying a multi-perspective approach can help to disentangle the processes at work and foster the understanding of for instance which foreign offenders will be deported after having completed their sentence and who is allowed to stay in the host country or of whether a certain applicant for naturalisation is finally accepted as a new citizen or not (cf. Achermann & Gass 2003).

Challenges of multi-perspective research

However, it is obvious that such a complex research design entails a number of difficulties and obstacles that we like to share with other researchers. First, it is a laborious and time-consuming way of doing research: a variety of actors needs to be contacted, informed, and convinced of participation; qualitative interviews take their time, and so does the collection of file information. Once data is collected, interviews need to be transcribed, collected information from files needs to be reordered and codified. A lack of time can lead to researchers not taking sufficient time to prepare the data collection well, including advance thinking and planning of the data processing. As gathering the data is considered to be the priority, there is a tendency of repressing the next stage when one would be very grateful for well prepared and structured data. Considering that qualitative research implies an explorative and inductive procedure, preparing in advance completely standardised databases for file analysis or for interview coding is neither possible nor to be aimed for. But still, keeping in mind that taking the time to plan well and try to structure as much as possible – leaving space and possibility for including information that does not fit into this frame – is surely worth it, especially when dealing with big quantities of data. This aspect is even more important if there is more emphasis on comparative aspects. In such a case a well prepared baseline study is needed in the course of which the research tools are developed and tested before starting to work on the other comparative cases. Another challenge related to time is not to lose sight of the fact that the possibilities to gather data are limited due to time and/or money constraints. As the multi-perspective approach actually aims at looking at 'everything' it can be difficult to define the moment where to stop data collection and make the point on the basis of what is at hand. Although risking not capturing as broad, as clear or as multifaceted a picture as intended, it is important to plan from the beginning the point of time when data collection is to be finished and analysis and writing of the report to be started. A second challenge to such an approach is the dependency on the access to all – or at least the most important – sources of data. If authorities or the management of the penitentiaries would not have agreed to cooperate and to grant access to files, to host us during almost two years of periodical data gathering and to let us conduct interviews with staff and inmates during working time, the realisation of the study would have been in serious peril.

Finally, when it comes to analysing the data and enacting what has been described to be the aims and advantages of the multi-perspective triangulation, there is another set of challenges waiting for the researcher: how is it possible to really treat the different perspectives in a balanced and just way? How to keep track of all the information and data in varying sources and formats? And how to analyse the details of the complex processes, elaborate what is happening and what the perspectives of the different actors are? As it might be typical for qualitative research, there is no general recipe, formula or computer programme that would guide researchers in this process. However, some basic rules might help others to find their way more easily through this jungle of information: At first an overview of the collected data has to be obtained and a system of how to order and classify needs to be developed. The idea of this is to know what kind of information has been gathered and to easily find the relevant details if needed. It can be useful to create a table or database with the key-variables for the analysis and fill in a résumé of the information from the varying sources. In the prison study this was mainly done with the information on inmates' socio-demographic characteristics, conviction and punishment, inclusion and exclusion from rehabilitation as well as preparation for release and on deportation or removal. Having classified data already before in a systematic manner facilitates the creation of such an overview considerably. However, when processing and analysing data it is important to remember that this overview is a superficial summary that is not thought to replace the details of the collected data. Rather, it should be considered to be a kind of guidepost leading to raw data which provide substance and illustration. When it comes to putting together different perspectives and keeping a balanced view, teamwork can be very useful and efficient in order to track the general outlines.

Doing research in penal institutions

After the sketch of the general approach, the focus will now be on the process of data collection in the particular context of two penitentiaries. There is a wide range of methodological and ethical questions that have to be solved before even entering a prison as a researcher, and more of them follow once the collection of data on the topic of foreign inmates is about to start. These experiences shall be shared with other researchers, especially those planning studies in the prison context.[13] Certain questions mentioned here are neither typical for the penal context nor exclusive to migration research. But both of these conditioning aspects structure in a very particular way the interactions and thereby define a specific context. There are mainly two areas where the peculiarities of migration research play an important role: on the one hand there is the precarious situation of the foreign national inmates: they are subject to multiple marginalisations by being at the same time incarcerated, criminal, foreign (and therefore deportable), often of low socio-economic status and frequently socially isolated. Lack of knowledge about the penal system and their rights, aggravated if they do not speak and understand the local language and the possible uncertainty concerning their deportation after release are further characteristics typical for non-national inmates. This not only affects their everyday life and therefore the topics to be treated in the interviews, but, as will be discussed later on, also asks for special sensitivity to and reflexivity towards power relations between researchers and the persons in the focus of the study. On the other hand, criminal foreigners are a sensitive topic, very often debated in an emotional way and instrumentalised for political purposes. Members of prison staff and management as well as of authorities tend to be very cautious in talking about this subject because they are not supposed to utter their personal political view and because of fear of either being blamed for discrimination or for doing harm to the foreign national inmates. This needs to be considered and asks for special proceeding in the course of preparation of the study but also when it comes to the publication of results. Sticking to a professional scientific attitude and working method seems of special importance in this case.

In the following three main aspects of doing research in penal institutions will be discussed: Getting access to the field of study, getting access to inmates as well as the relation between researchers and researched, and finally the personal coping of the researcher in this area of study.

Access to prisons

Unless s/he commits a crime, it is not an easy thing to get into a prison as a researcher.[14] Penal institutions are not only well protected to prevent inmates from escaping but also towards outsiders wanting to enter. Especially closed penitentiaries with high security-standards are highly controlled organisations where deviations from the normal order are first of all considered to be a risk and to cause problems. Even if the final decision to participate in the study lies with the head of the responsible administration, the first hurdle to take is to gain trust and interest by the prison management.[15] Besides presenting a research project that is thoroughly done and of a certain relevance to the prison, too, personal meetings to get to know each other are an indispensable precondition for a good start. Pre-existing contacts to the management facilitate this process a great deal. The main task is to convince that research will be done carefully, that the rules (especially of security and data protection) and the special logic of the institution will be respected and that no trouble will be caused, apart from some efforts connected to the data gathering. In our case, once the directors of the two prisons had agreed to support our study, they granted us full confidence and great room for manoeuvre, opened us their gates whenever we wanted, helped us in organising the interviews, gave us access to their archives for file analysis, etc. The only limits to our freedom as researchers were security concerns. Such precautions however were intended to protect us from possible harm and were not an expression of mistrust. An example for this was that contrary to lawyers we were never expected to pass the metal detector at the entrance of the prison.

Besides adhering to security rules we were expected to respect concerns related to protection of privacy of the inmates. A contract subjecting us to strict duties concerning data and privacy protection was signed at the very beginning of the study with both of the prisons and the administrative services. In that respect we were considered equal to staff so that in our presence people did not need to be cautious giving names of inmates or to hide documents containing personal information. As far as members of staff were concerned, for them this was another symbol that we could be considered trustworthy. Apart from respecting the privacy of the inmates, the managements were also concerned with their basic rights in general. Regarding our study this meant in the first sense that they would have to voluntarily agree to an interview. Whereas for us as researchers it was evident that it would not only be unethical but also completely useless to oblige persons – inmates as well as members of staff – to participate in an interview, the managements' concern was mainly to avoid accusations of having forced inmates to participate. In order to prevent this, before beginning the interview every inmate had to sign a form in which s/he declared to participate voluntarily and thereby expressed his/her informed consent.

The fact that our study had not been funded or mandated as an evaluation study by a public service somehow connected to, or even in charge of, the penitentiaries turned out to be an advantage. Even if this was not that much of a deliberate choice, the fact that the project was financed as part of a larger programme promoting fundamental research (cf. above) probably facilitated access to the institutions as well as to interview partners. The advantages of this background were twofold: In the potentially sensitive context of foreigners and prisons where fears of being controlled and blamed for doing something wrong are considerable – not least because very often these are the only occasions when prisons attract public interest –, it was of great use to make credible that our work was independent, scientific and not linked to any immediate political mandate. For the interviewed members of staff and management this facilitated talking openly because they would be less concerned that, based on their statements, changes in their institution would be decided on or that there could be negative consequences for themselves. For us as researchers it was an advantage too: we were clearly in the position of outsiders to the entire penal system (cf. Waldram 1998: 240) and appreciated that we could just step into these organisations and start to discover them as if we were 'aliens'. Another advantage was that we did not have to struggle with problems of accountability towards a sponsor and his ideas of how to conduct our research. Thereby we did not encounter the kind of problems Waldram (1998: 242) describes for the case of a proposed – and finally refused – contract research where the correctional officials would have had to be granted access to all original records and data including the revelation of the informants' identities.

Access to interview partners in prisons and establishing rapport

Once access to the prison and the possibility to do interviews is granted, the next hurdles to take are first to find inmates and staff who are ready to give an interview. Second, as most scientific literature on prison research highlights, 'establishing rapport' (Patenaude 2004) and gaining trust are crucial to create an interview situation in which an open and trustful interaction can take place. Both tasks include a number of ethical but also methodological aspects that need to be considered in order to comply with scientific standards.

Preparations: Sampling and willingness to participate

When preparing interviews in the prison context researchers have to be aware of some particularities of this area that are not as obvious at first sight as are security concerns. For instance, it is important to bear in mind that inmates as well as members of staff of prison are marginal groups with weak social prestige and with hardly any lobby defending their interests. This entails one negative and one positive consequence: Inmates and members of staff are generally suspicious towards outsiders and critical about what they want from them. Researchers therefore have to gain their interest and respect. The positive side of this marginal situation is that prisons are rather rarely researched organisations[16] and that their members may be happy about the interest in them and therefore be open to participation. A second aspect is that penal institutions are by definition characterised by strong power hierarchy, coercion and limited autonomy of the inmates. As mentioned above, due to their multiple marginalization foreign prisoners might be or feel even stronger affected by this condition than national inmates. Researchers need to be aware of this context, but at the same time have to bear in mind that they are not part of these power relations themselves. In other words: it is not researchers' task to take part in the enacting of the prison's duties towards the inmates or in supporting inmates to withdraw from these constraining conditions, but rather to observe and try to understand what is going on and take these relations to be a topic for study.

Being sensitive to power relations can interfere with researchers' aims to choose a balanced sample and to attain a given number of interview partners. In order to achieve exactly the sample planned the selected inmates could be obliged to participate. However, as it has been mentioned above, both for ethical and methodological reasons participation in interviews has to be voluntary. For our study we chose two different approaches to mobilising inmates to participate in the interviews: in the female prison we invited[17] all of the foreign inmates to information events in the section where they lived and informed them personally about who we were, what we planned to do and what an interview would imply.[18] Those interested in participating were asked to fill in a form. This first round of information and mobilising was a crucial moment for the whole project as we had absolutely no idea whether the inmates would be willing to talk to us or not. If they were not this would have been a serious problem for our research design. It was a positive surprise however that more than half (27) of the total foreign inmate population (48) was ready to give us an interview. It seems that Waldram's observation that the inmates seized the 'offer to consent to, and meaningfully participate in, the research as an opportunity to express their limited autonomy' (1998: 241) corresponds to our own experience. Apart from the voluntary interest to participate no other criteria was applied for the sample of female inmates to be interviewed. We were lucky that we managed to have a broad range of different situations represented, although there were quite a large number of Brazilian drug traffickers and no foreign inmate of the second generation among them. Concerning the big group of Brazilians it was evident and we were told by the management too that we could not turn down inmates once they had decided they wanted to participate. For the second group of the *'secondas'* we tried to convince some of these inmates but they refused because, among other things, they did not feel part of the group of 'foreign inmates'.

Based on this first experience of considerable interest in working with us we adapted our strategy for the male prison. As the absolute number of foreign inmates was much higher (146) and we did not have the time to interview all of them, we made a first choice of inmates to be invited to an information event. This choice was based on theoretical sampling striving for a broad representation of different situations as far as origin, legal status, age, duration of sentence, and duration of stay in prison was concerned. The offence itself was no criterion of choice.[19] The procedure of informing and signing on corresponded to the one in the female prison except for informing (in German, English and French) all of the invited inmates at the same time in the assembly hall. Here too, there was big interest in our study: out of 35 invited inmates 33 participated in the information meeting and 31 finally filled in the form.[20]

For the interviews with members of staff, the procedure was slightly different: after having informed the staff on what we were doing, we communicated to the management with how many collaborators of which divisions of the prison we wanted to talk to. Thereafter, we were given a plan of persons being willing and available the days the interviews were done. It seemed that members of staff had not been obliged to participate, however contrary to the inmates there might have been more pressure and expectation on them to agree. As regards to this aspect of voluntary participation in the institutional setting of the penitentiary as well as in qualitative research in general, it is obvious that staff as well as inmates may not have decided completely freely to participate because they could have expected either positive consequences of presenting themselves or negative consequences if not doing so. Researchers cannot entirely control such dynamics. From an ethical perspective however it is important that also during the interview persons are not pushed or even constrained to tell things and give information. Considering interviewees – even in the coercive context of a prison – as powerful, reasonable and responsible actors who have the choice to decide on what they want to tell in the interview and what they want to keep to themselves we tried to be alert to any expression of such refusal.

Another important task during the preparation of the interviews was to gain respect, of the inmates as well as of the members of staff. We thought that would be the first step towards gaining trust during the interview. The number of people showing interest in having an interview illustrates the importance of our strategy of informing inmates on what our research project was about in an open and understandable way (including translation). It demonstrated that we were independent and could be trusted in.

Still, it was obvious that the foreign inmates were not only willing to talk to us because they were convinced of the importance of our research and that we were trustworthy persons. The simple fact that the interviews would take place during working hours and would be an occasion to talk to an unknown man and a woman for two hours, maybe even with a translator, must have been a big incentive for many of them.

Participation in the interview: opening up, building trust, and interaction between interviewees and researchers

Agreeing to give an interview does not mean that the person in question automatically talks in an open way and that a trustful atmosphere develops between the interviewee and the researcher. The way the first interactions and the beginning of the cooperation happened certainly influences the interview. But building up an open and confidential interaction during the interview in which the informant talks freely about what s/he thinks, does and feels is part of the interviewer's work.[21] As far as foreign national inmates are concerned, creating trust can be a different process if we compare it with other inmates. It is possible that out of fear or earlier experienced lack of respect, abuse or discrimination they do not trust anybody in the prison context as principle (see also Barsky in this book). But it is also possible, and rather corresponds to our experiences, that they are less suspicious because most of them will be deported upon release and as such they are not afraid of being recognised in public.

The general conditions of the interview that determine the first impressions are important aspects that should not be neglected: the location where the interviews take place deserves some reflection. We did our interviews in rooms familiar to most of the inmates: in the visitors' room in the female prison and the room where inmates meet advocates or priests in the male prison. The fact that these were positively known places to the inmates where they have lived moments of privacy before was certainly an advantage. As two researchers were present at every interview, the seating order was important in order to prevent the inmate from finding him-/herself facing a 'row' of researchers, almost like facing a court. Another point was that the inmates would sit with their back to a door with a window in it in order to avoid him/her being distracted or feeling that other people could be present.

For the interviews we did with an interpreter, besides the usual challenges to translated interviews (e.g. interaction between three parties, control of the interview, not being able to check the quality of translation) for the prison context we had to consider additional aspects: first, translators had to be accepted by the prison management and sign a contract of data protection as well. Second, we had to brief them well, find solutions for some of their fears (e.g. one translator did not want the inmates to get to know his real name) and especially ensure that the translator would not be a danger to a trustful interview atmosphere because of the influence of his/her own attitudes. Particularly with rather small linguistic groups in a given country, privacy and data protection can be a problem as the translator and the interviewee risk knowing each other or having common acquaintances.[22]

With regard to confidentiality of the interviews it was obvious to everyone that they were not completely anonymous as it was generally known which inmates and which members of staff did participate. Because of this we told the interviewees that if they wanted to tell us something that should in no way be related to their person they should tell and we would treat this information with special caution. This means that in publications such information can neither be quoted nor be contextualised by relating it to characteristics of the informant like his/her origin, age or – in the case of members of staff – their function. Interviewees were asked if they agreed to us recording the interview, what can be considered to be a first test if they really trusted us. Only one member of staff (out of 35) and one inmate (out of 60) refused the recording. Some members of staff however asked at a certain point in the conversation to turn the recorder off because they were giving confidential or delicate information. With others we realised that off the record – e.g. during breaks for smoking outside the interview room or after the interview – they talked in a different, more informal way naming problems more openly.

Besides such general conditions of the interview, the personal interaction between interviewee and researcher is crucial for the outcome of the interview. Nowadays, it is broadly acknowledged in qualitative research that personal characteristics of researchers (e.g. gender, age, language, socio-economic status) influence the way interviewees react and respond. Instead of trying to eliminate this influence there is some common sense that reflecting status differences and power relations between researchers and interviewees might be more important and also of more use. This is especially true when working with people in precarious conditions and when the status differences and power hierarchy between the two actors are particularly large. Our case of Swiss researchers living in freedom interviewing foreign national prison inmates is certainly an example of such a situation. So what to do about it? On the one hand merely being aware of such differences and their effects during the interview and when analysing data seems to be crucial. This means that it is important to consider and deal cautiously with aspects of power and status differences in order to prevent from doing harm to the persons under study but also from distortions of the results due to misunderstandings. On the other hand, special emphasis might be given to building up trust and to overcome social distance during the interview.[23] A first step to do this is to encounter the interviewees as responsible and reasonable actors. Part of this is to tell them in an open and transparent way what the study is about, what will result from it and what the position and task of the researcher is. Inmates as well as members of staff should understand that the researcher is not on a particular side of any of the actors, but that s/he is listening to all of them and trying to understand what is happening how and why.

When it comes to creating trust, qualitative interviews are certainly well suited as their open and less standardised character leaves room to consider the individual, to accord him the possibility to bring in his/her own topics and to tell 'his story' or to focus on certain topics. By this the interviewee is granted certain autonomy, given room to talk and thereby shown respect and taken seriously.[24] This is a way of fostering a trustful talk that most interviewees appreciate and profit from. Liebling (1999: 155) points to one lesson she had learned when doing interviews with prisoners: 'how obliging staff and prisoners can be, and how open to interested outsiders', which exactly corresponds to our experience. But also researchers need to be open, interested, unbiased and above all empathic in order to contribute to a good atmosphere of open speech. In the case of prison inmates this could be difficult: how to be empathic with someone who committed a crime? An important aspect facilitating to meet interviewees without any prejudices and an unbiased attitude was that we did not know at that point what offence they were in prison for.[25] This way, it was easier to get to know the inmates in the first sense as persons with their particular stories, and not as offenders. Some of them talked about their offence in the course of the interview – mostly if it was not related to physical violence or if they presented themselves as being innocent – others never mentioned it. Because of our main research interest in the present life in the penal institution and in the inmates' future we did not need to ask about their (criminal) past if they did not mention it. It was obvious that the inmates appreciated our interviews especially because for once they could talk for up to two hours to outsiders who were only interested in themselves as persons and not in what kind of offence they had committed.

Nevertheless, there is a second side of the coin in creating trustful relations to interviewees: there is a danger for the researchers of losing distance, of getting involved and touched too much by the stories and fate of the inmates. Discussing an 'anthropology of prisons', Rhodes (2001: 76) highlights that '[t]o forget one's position as an outsider is to be in danger, not only from interpersonal trouble of various kinds but, more enduringly from emotional and intellectual identifications'. The more an informant opens up and shows emotions – tears were frequent, especially when asking about their families – the more difficult it gets to keep what is called 'professional distance' (cf. below). As the researcher might be one of the first persons the foreign inmate has talked to in such a way since s/he entered the prison, even within the short period of time of the interview a kind of closeness can develop between the two parties. This is especially true for foreign nationals who tend not to be visited on a regular basis. In this situation the researcher has to try to keep the balance between gaining trust, showing empathy, but still keeping a needed distance and being transparent to the inmates with regard to what s/he can do for them and what is not possible. Foreign inmates very often not having many contacts to Swiss (apart from staff), there is a considerable danger of them hoping or even expecting researchers to be able to help them in one way or the other, be it to get out of prison, not to be deported, to be granted prison leave or to get a – in their perspective – fair trial. But not only inmates expect researchers to be on their side, the same is true for members of staff. Whereas for inmates it is the interest taken in them and the built up trust that is the main ground for taking for granted that the researcher takes a stand for them, in case of staff it might rather be the common nationality and the fact of being non-criminals that makes them expect the researchers to be on their side. However, some members of staff rather thought, probably because of the focus of our study, that we were on the foreign inmates' side, wanted to defend them and therefore were suspicious of our unbiased attitude (cf. Liebling 1999: 168). Some of them revised their view while talking to us, others probably never really trusted that we were striving for a balanced view.

The topic of expectations leads to another ethical question that had to be solved: what can researchers return for the information, trust and openness they receive from inmates? Of course, this is no new question to any person gathering data in social sciences. However, interviewing marginalised persons who not only mostly lack interest, recognition and respect but also dispose of limited economic and social resources, this question is even more important and needs serious reflection. In our case, as an explicit sign of gratitude and reciprocity, all the inmates we interviewed were sent a short letter thanking them and a phone card they could use to call from the prison. Besides, we told them to make public in our research reports their point of view and thereby 'give them a voice'.[26] Additionally, some people asked us for information on practical or administrative things we were able to explain and thereby giving something back to them. But as it became evident after some interviews, probably the most important thing we could give was our interest, respect and recognition as human beings. The overwhelming majority of the inmates expressed their gratitude for this at the end of the interviews, some in extensive and almost formal speeches. Some even wanted to invite us to their cell in order to offer us a cup of tea. And a few sent us letters thanking us for the interview and our little gift.[27]

Once the interviews finished, other ethical concerns had to be solved: as outlined above, we intended to complement our view by analysing not only interviews but also inmates' files. We thought about asking inmates for their consent to do this, finally renounced to it because of two reasons: first, there were some doubts if inmates would still trust us or if they would misunderstand this as being a way to control whether they were telling the truth in the interviews. Second, as we were analysing a great number of files most of which were about persons that had already been released, it would have been strange to ask some of the inmates for their consent and others not. Finally, we came to the conclusion that when reading the files after the interviews, the inmates would not be concerned and it would not cause any harm to them. Other researchers in similar contexts tell about dilemmas of another type: what to do with so called 'dirty information', i.e. information on which difficult decisions on how to use it have to be made (Thomas & Marquart 1987)? In none of our interviews we were confronted to such kind of information. However, when doing research in areas like prisons one should be prepared to getting to know things that can have an effect on you as a researcher but that also can damage the informants if they should become public.[28]

Personal coping as a researcher

Doing interviews in potentially stressing environments like penitentiaries and with people living in difficult situations can be hard to cope with for researchers. Surprisingly enough, such aspects are rarely talked about or mentioned in scientific literature. It seems as if in science people doing research do not exist as human beings but merely as researchers, anthropologists, sociologists, etc. However, as Liebling (1999) points out in an article on doing research in the penal context we can and should not forget that we are at the same time researchers and human beings with subjective feelings. Instead of pretending to be a tool to make us forget our human part, methodology should rather serve for taking into account these emotional aspects and dealing with them consciously. In the study on foreign national inmates in closed prisons there were three set of challenges concerning these questions of personal coping that shall be discussed in the following.

First, the balance between 'professional distance' and showing empathy can be a problem. Liebling stresses that their 'interviews were frequently very emotional, for interviewer and interviewee alike. Often, we emerged from these encounters exhausted, upset, occasionally uplifted' (1999: 158). Interviewing prisoners can provoke two kinds of emotional reactions: compassion with a sad or tragic story or repudiation towards what the interviewee has done. Typically, a researcher would be expected to stay neutral, to keep a professional distance and not to show any emotions. However, such a demand is contradictory to the need for creating a trustful atmosphere in which the researchers show empathy and try to take the perspective of the interviewees so that these would tell what their lives, fears and other feelings are about. Such challenges to researchers of opening and still keeping a distance are not exclusive to the prison experience and to migration research. However, due to their often isolated situations people in precarious situations might be more likely to seize such an opportunity for baring their soul to the researcher listening empathically.

Based on our experiences, two aspects seem to be important in dealing with this balancing act: on the one hand, during the interview we tried to show compassion, patience, and listen. Sometimes, being interested and trying to understand the interviewee's point of view was the closest we were able to get to being comprehensive. Very emotional situations (e.g. sadness, anger, desperation) need their time before going ahead with other interview questions. However, it is crucial not to lose control of the interview. As Liebling (1999: 156) describes there can be situations where researchers are asked or expected to help in a given situation and take action. Here too, the challenge is to keep the balance between on the one hand sticking to the role of the researcher who does not advocate for the interviewed and helping within predefined and transparently communicated limits on the other hand. For instance, if asked for, we did give advice concerning whom a person can turn to in a difficult situation or with urgent questions. But we refrained from taking concrete action as well as from taking a stand on questions like if something was right or wrong or if the inmate had been convicted rightfully or not. On the other hand, after the interview it was important to think and discuss about our experiences and personal reactions. For such a kind of debriefing, doing interviews in pairs is of great help. However, as Liebling highlights, discussing in the research team in an open way and explicitly referring to subjective feelings is not only important for personal coping, but also for interpreting and understanding: '[O]ur emotions do not need to be reconciled with our so-called data. They constitute data. They require critical reflection and triangulation, and 'faithful representation', but not selective inattention. [. . .] [R]eflexivity with an ethic seems to me to provide a way of tackling the emotional dimension of research honestly and with some purpose' (1999: 164).

The second challenge is specific to the multi-perspective research approach: working with diverse sources of data can imply two difficulties concerning personal coping. As we looked at inmates' files after the interviews we experienced some surprises in getting to know another side of the persons we had talked to. As the great majority of the interviews were done in a very open, comfortable, and mutually respectful way, the sometimes shocking stories of the offences these same persons had committed was a confusing experience. For instance, there was one man with whom I had a very interesting and reflective talk about life in prison. When I read his file and learnt that he had raped a young woman, I ended up quite confused and found it hard to imagine that the man I had talked to and the one I read about in the files were the same person. This somehow upsetting experience concerned the research or data collection only as far as it confirmed the importance of having separated and sequenced the two information sources, i.e. of not having seen the files before doing the interviews. Moreover, it was mainly a point to deal with and a reason to reflect upon individually and as a team for instance on the challenges to our ideas of what is 'good' or 'evil', but also on what our reactions tell us that could be useful for the understanding of the research topic.

Another difficulty related to the multi-perspective research approach was to take into account and do interviews with different actors involved. Obviously, staff, inmates and members of authorities had quite different views on certain questions. Although this makes it very interesting to analyse, while doing interviews the researcher can, to a certain point, feel divided because s/he tries to put him-/herself into the different situations and tries to understand all of the perspectives described. Here again, being conscious of such impressions, noting them down and reflecting upon them, including possible influences on the way the interview was done is very important. Conducting interviews with different groups of actors separately and if possible even with some time in-between the interview blocks can facilitate the distancing of the view of a given group and make it easier to be open again to get to know the other 'side'.[29]

The third challenge concerning personal coping is the danger of 'going native'. Even if we did not do 'proper' participant observation in the sense of participating in prison life for a long period of time, there were two incidents that made me realise that I and my perspective had changed: first, one morning when coming to the female prison in order to continue work in the archive, the security officer at the gate welcomed me, knew my name and told me that after all the time I was already almost a part of 'them'. Second, in the course of another research project I once went to visit a detention centre for foreigners. Afterwards, I talked to an anthropologist who had been at the same place recently. Whereas to me it was mainly 'another prison', with some particularities and many commonalities that were familiar and somehow 'normal', the colleague being a 'prison-newcomer' was quite upset and somehow even shocked after having seen the inmates, the cells and locked doors, the gangways of cells and all the other characteristics and symbols of the coercive conditions of imprisonment. As Liebling (1999: 163) writes, 'the risks of 'going native' are high – particularly when long periods of time are spent with staff and prisoners in the 'deep end' of prison life'. The two incidents made me realise that I had started to really become part of the two institutions and the 'prison world'. The question then is what researchers should do when they get to that point: leave the field because we are losing distance? Or is this actually the point where we start to know the context, its rules and the significances really well and therefore begin to understand what is happening? Probably both parts are true in a way. However, more important in this sense seems to be that the researcher does not get involved to the point of really identifying with the subject and that s/he keeps the ability of reflecting what is happening to him-/herself, records these experiences and takes them into account for the analysis. However, before being able to analyse data properly, it is necessary to gain back distance to the field of the penitentiary as well as to its actors in order to really apply a balanced multi-perspective research approach.

Lessons learnt and what to change the next time

To finish I would like to point out what I would change next time when conducting a similar research. A first point concerns the group of inmates to be interviewed. If possible the group of inmates taken into account for the interviews should be enlarged in two senses: on the one hand possibilities would have to be found how to attain broader sampling of (especially the female) inmates. The challenge would mainly be how to reach those foreign national inmates that had been born or had grown up in Switzerland and who did not consider themselves as belonging to the group of 'foreign inmates'. Specific and adapted ways of inviting and informing this and/or other groups that are hard to reach would have to be found and applied. On the other hand if at all possible (as regards to the financial resources of the project) national inmates should be included into the research as well. There were some Swiss inmates asking us why they had been excluded from the interviews and who did not understand the reasons for this choice (actually being purely pragmatic due to lack of money and time). Rather, they took it as a confirmation that once more the majority of the foreign inmates did get more attention and special treatment compared to them. Doing interviews with a sample of all inmates (national and foreign) would add another perspective on life in prison and contribute to, among other things, differentiate what is particular to foreign inmates and what might be typical for all kind of inmates, independent of their nationality. In contrast, the particular focus on the migration topic and sampling in this logic can result in a restricted view on the prison as a whole.

A second point concerns participant observation that has hardly been mentioned up to now due to the focus on the interviews. Although it was not possible to do 'real' participant observation over a prolonged period of time, we spent a lot of time in the prisons while collecting our data (interviews and file research) and had a lot of occasions to observe interactions and ethnographic details. Even while sitting in a room next to the secretary and just noticing the daily routines, when eating in the cafeteria with staff or when crossing inmates going to or coming from work we learnt a lot about how these organisations work, how people behave within them, and what effects the organisations have on people living and working in them. Such observations were recorded in field notes. Besides, there were many occasions where we too realised the restricted mobility in a prison – if for instance you depend on a guard opening doors for you even for such basic needs as going to a toilet.[30]

But still, being able to participate more and having more occasions for informal talks to all members of the penitentiary would certainly have enriched data and deepened our understanding. Looking at it retrospectively it could have been worth asking the prison management for doing participant observation once again after they had got to know us and the way we were working and after we had got to know the institution with its rules and modus operandi as well as some inmates and members of staff. In the literature on prison ethnography there are some examples of researchers who managed by different means to do participant observation in penitentiaries: Jones (1995) being an inmate himself, Fleisher (1989) working as a guardian, and Le Caisne (2000) got into the prison as a trainee for two weeks and then prolonged her stay as a researcher for two years. If the first two examples raise ethical concerns as regards to 'undercover research', the latter is confronted with a problem Rhodes (2001: 76) hints to: 'no outsider/ observer can 'participate' in the situation of the prisoner'.

Conclusion

This chapter is not about giving recipes or presenting best practice on doing migration research in the prison context. It aims much more at sharing experiences and reflecting on methodology and ethics with other researchers in order to make ourselves aware of possible pitfalls and to encourage thinking beforehand about strategies for challenges to appear. The underlying epistemological attitude is the Weberian (1968) idea of social sciences aiming at 'interpretive understanding' and explanation of social action that asks for an adequate methodology and includes ethical considerations.

The multi-perspective research approach used in a study on foreign national inmates in closed Swiss prisons intents to understand in the most comprehensive way what the phenomenon of a majority of foreign prisoners in the two penal institutions is about, what it implies and to find explanations for why things are happening in a given way. Besides the potentials of this broad, deep and complex research design taking into account not only the perspective of a variety of actors but also diverse types of data, difficulties are discussed as well. A major problem of such an approach is that working with multiple partners and diverse data is rather time consuming: there has to be a base for cooperation with several organisations built up, their own logic has to be understood, qualitative data collection itself takes time, etc. Teamwork therefore is almost indispensable, also in order to be able to keep a balanced view, triangulate the different perspectives and data and validate interpretations.

The interaction between researchers and researched foreign inmates as well as members of staff mainly in the course of the interviews is given special attention. Focussing on how to get access to the institution and to the persons themselves, the question is how interest and trust can be gained and what difficulties for instance concerning interviewees' expectations towards interviewers can arise. Another aspect of this rapport between researchers and researched concerns the very often unmentioned questions of how to cope as a researcher with the potentially emotionally stressing consequences of working with people in precarious conditions. Here again, working in a team is an important resource for personal coping as well as for making subjective experiences useful for scientific purposes.

As regards to methodological and ethical questions in migration research more generally, the following aspects can be highlighted as a summary:

- It is important that researchers respect in a balanced way both their responsibility towards scientific interests on the one hand and responsibility towards the people they study (be they migrants, prison staff or authorities) on the other hand. Applying a multi-perspective design can be an attempt to satisfy both of these demands by trying to understand a complex phenomenon in its diversity and complexity and to embrace and do justice to the multiple perspectives of the actors involved.
- The example of the prison study showed the importance of considering the vulnerability of migrants as well as the potential political sensitivity of migration topics from staff or authorities' point of view. Personal contacts in the preparation of data collection to both groups of actors in order to build up trust is one important part of this. Anyway, trust turned out to be a key concept on which most of the data collection and therefore the execution of the study depends. Thinking about the methodological question of how to gain it and the ethical duty of not abusing it are of paramount importance in contexts considered to be sensitive due to precarious situations and/or anxieties of the actors involved.
- A third challenge that is common to qualitative research with marginalised groups – for instance also with undocumented migrants – is to keep the balance between involvement and distance in relation to the field and the actors of the study. Persons otherwise having few

resources tend to consider researchers they got to know as being trustful and understanding as part of their personal network. Consequently, they might expect them for instance to help or become friends. How to limit and deal with such expectations in a personally, ethically and methodologically responsible way should be reflected on before starting data collection.

Applying, testing and modifying the presented multi-perspective approach with regards to other research topics and sharing such experiences would be of great interest and a possibility to continue reflection on how to cope with methodological and ethical challenges migration research can be confronted with. Interdisciplinary exchange with other fields having to find strategies for questions like balance between involvement and distance, status differences, and personal coping (e.g. psychology, psychiatry, social work) could provide additional inputs for dealing with these challenges in research projects (see also introduction of this book) and thereby add another dimension to multi-perspective research.

Acknowledgement

I would like to thank Ueli Hostettler and Stefanie Gass with whom I did the two research projects this chapter is based on. Most of the experiences described in this chapter were made in teamwork with one or the other of them and I am grateful for the very good collaboration and the many discussions we had on all types of questions related to scientific work, not least of the methodological and ethical kind. I also thank Ueli Hostettler, Joëlle Moret and the reviewers for helpful comments and critical remarks on an earlier version of this chapter.

Notes

1   Swiss Federal Office of Statistics, imprisonment statistics as at 8th February 2007.
2   See for early articles on the topic Baechtold (2000) and Wicker (2002).
3   The project 'Foreigners in Closed Swiss Prisons: Issues of their Management and the Problem of Resocialisation in the Context of National Law, Migration Control, and Transnational Mobility' was funded by the Swiss National Science Foundation in its National Research Programme 51 'Social Integration and Social Exclusion'. The study was conceptualised and guided by Hans-Rudolf Wicker (Institute of Social Anthropology, University of Bern), project collaborators were Christin Achermann, Ueli Hostettler and Jonas Weber (legal expert). Research was carried out between September 2003 and August 2005. Cf. more details: http://www.nfp51.ch/e_module. cfm?Slanguage=e&get=32&Projects.Command=details.
4   'Unerwünscht' is the term used in the foreign nationals act as in force until the end of the year 2007. The new law does not use this term anymore.
5   See for an overview of the Swiss penal system the article by Baechtold (2001)

and the publication by the Federal Office of Justice (2006) (http://www.bj.admin.ch/etc/medialib/data/sicherheit/straf_und_massnahmen /documentation.Par.0006.File.tmp/smv-ch-e.pdf).

6 For an example of some strategies of that type in British prisons see the report by the HM Inspectorate of Prisons (2006) and the handbook for foreign national prisoners by HM Prison Service (2004).

7 For more results of the overall research see Achermann (2008) and Achermann & Hostettler (2006, 2007).

8 Goffman (1961a, 1961b) opposes these two groups as belonging to two distinct 'worlds' thereby stressing the different roles and conditions.

9 Another possibility for taking into account the inmates' views would be to collect information not by face-to-face interaction but by written testimonies sent to the researchers by mail (Bosworth et al. 2005). This could be especially useful if access to the penitentiary is not granted. However, as letters might be checked by staff, confidentiality of the information transmitted can hardly be guaranteed.

10 About a third of all interviews were done with the help of interpreters for the following languages: Albanian, Arab, Brazilian Portuguese, Kurdish, Tamil, and Turkish.

11 Two of these interviews were done with staff of the prison department of the Canton of Zurich, the rest with administrative staff from the Canton of Bern.

12 Out of these 60 files were analysed in depth. The others mainly provided information on the legal status of the inmates.

13 See Patenaude (2004) for an article discussing qualitative research 'within correctional contexts' in the U.S. The author being a former correctional officer, he was confronted with specific challenges and advantages: 'My previous status as a correctional officer was a concern akin to a double-edged sword; it was believed that it could increase rapport with the staff ranks (correctional officers and treatment staff), yet it could also decrease any such rapport among those inmates being studied if care was not taken to show a lack of bias' (Patenaude 2004: 77s).

14 Jones (1995) gives an example of a prison study he did while himself being an inmate in a maximum security prison for one year. He describes it as a 'unique approach to the study of prisons, an ethnographic study that utilised a complete participant (inmate-sociologist) and an outside observer (sociology professor) as a way of achieving an insider's understanding while maintaining an outsider's objectivity' (Jones 1995: 106).

15 Switzerland has no review boards, ethical committees or similar institutions for social sciences that have to approve a study for instance on vulnerable populations as prisoners are normally considered to be.

16 Wacquant (2002: 387) supposes that the low social status of prisons and inmates as objects of study is one reason for the 'curious eclipse of prison ethnography in the age of mass incarceration'. However, I think the main reasons for the scarce ethnographic research in penal institutions are mainly to be sought in (supposed) difficulties of access and in personal reservation towards confrontation with offenders and penitentiaries.

17 All of the foreign national inmates were handed out a written invitation in German, Portuguese, English, French or Spanish.

18 As there was a considerable number of Brazilian inmates at that time, we were accompanied by a Brazilian Portuguese-speaking interpreter already at these information events.

19 However, on the lists our choice was made on, the offences were noted as well. In general, we did not pay attention to this information. Nevertheless, one inmate who was among the first choice of potential interviewees and who had been sentenced for paedophilic deeds was excluded because of the objection of one interviewer.

20 While doing the interviews, we accepted two more persons who expressed their will to participate as well. Due to time reasons we had to refuse further inmates who would also have been interested.

21 How the interviewees experience the interview as such and what the questions asked by the researcher can trigger is hardly known and discussed. The article by Bosworth et al. (2005) that is co-authored by a researcher and four inmates deals with the 'views from inside' and with the 'emotional nature of being part of a study and how a researcher gains participants' trust' (Bosworth et al. 2005: 249).

22 Translators should be instructed beforehand to tell the researchers if they find out that they know the interviewee. This way they can decide together if the interview should be postponed and done with another translator.

23 Bourdieu (1997: 784, 787f) emphasises this point and the way different positions of interviewers and informants in the social space can create distortions. He therefore pleads for taking into account both the individual story and fate and its particular social context. Furthermore, he suggests using interviewers of the same social field as the interviewees in order to enable a kind of 'natural conversation' and proper mutual understanding. Besides general doubts on this last proposal, in the case of prisons it would not have been possible to apply such a method.

24 Using qualitative interview methods therefore can be a way of taking into account the inmates' perspective without needing to integrate inmates into the process of preparing questionnaires as Waldram (1998) did in order to 'empower' aboriginal inmates.

25 As it has been mentioned above when making the choice of the persons to be invited we had seen their offences on the list. However we were neither able to nor interested in remembering this information once we started the interviewing.

26 Such a promise however can cause ethical dilemmas if for different reasons (time, finding publisher, and teamwork) the publication of data takes time or is realised only partially.

27 For instance, one man wrote to us that in the course of the 8 years and 9 months since he has been imprisoned he had never received such a kind letter as we had sent him. He was supposed to spend another three years in prison for having killed his wife.

28 Thomas and Marquart point to the fact that researchers will have to decide whether to act honourably or ethically, i.e. to avoid shame or guilt: 'The relationship between proper behaviour and managing dirty information is paradoxical. [. . .] By definition, paradoxes have no ready solution' (1987: 91).

29   Thomas and Marquart (1987) discuss the difficulty of doing the right thing for every 'audience' mainly as far as the publication of information is concerned. They highlight that it is mostly impossible to make everyone happy. However, it is up to the researcher to decide what according to him/her the ethical or the honourable choice is. Waldram on the other hand argues that an anthropologist should take a stand and empower and protect vulnerable populations as for instance aboriginal inmates because of their lack of power (Waldram 1998). Based on our experiences the most important task of the researchers is to find a way to deal respectfully with the data collected based on trust obtained from informants' while at the same time writing a report without censorship and without sparing certain actors, but presenting results that are based on scientifically collected and analysed data.

30   See for similar experiences Liebling (1999: 160) who writes: 'We lived, albeit temporarily, in circumstances reminiscent of the prison experience – without easy access to telephones, away from our friends, cut off from our lives, and propelled into others' worlds, with all the consequences staff reported to us of prolonged detached duty'.

Bibliography

Achermann, C. (2008), *Straffällig, unerwünscht, ausgeschlossen: Ausländische Strafgefangene in der Schweiz.* Dissertation an der Philosophisch-historischen Fakultät der Universität Bern. Bern: Selbstverlag.

Achermann, C. & S. Gass (2003), *Staatsbürgerschaft und soziale Schliessung: Eine rechtsethnologische Sicht auf die Einbürgerungspraxis der Stadt Basel.* Zürich: Seismo.

Achermann, C. & U. Hostettler (2006), 'AusländerIn ist nicht gleich AusländerIn: Strafvollzugsalltag und Entlassungsvorbereitung einer vielfältigen Insassengruppe', in Riklin, F. (Ed.), *Straffällige ohne Schweizerpass: Kriminalisieren – Entkriminalisieren – Exportieren? Délinquants sans passeport suisse: Criminaliser, décriminaliser, exporter?*, 21–35. Luzern: Caritas Schweiz/ Fachgruppe 'Reform im Strafwesen'.

Achermann, C. & U. Hostettler (2007), 'Femmes et hommes en milieu pénitentiaire fermé en Suisse: Aspects genre et migration', *Nouvelles Questions Féministes*, 26 (1): 70–88.

Baechtold, A. (2000), 'Strafvollzug und Strafvollstreckung an Ausländern: Prüfstein der Strafrechtspflege oder bloss 'suitable enemies'?', *Schweizerische Zeitschrift für Strafrecht*, 118 (3): 245–269.

Baechtold, A. (2001), 'Switzerland', in van Zyl Smit, D. & F. Dünkel (eds.), *Imprisonment Today and Tomorrow: International Perspectives on Prisoners' Rights and Prison Conditions*: 653–675. The Hague: Kluwer Law International.

Bosworth, M., D. Campbell, B. Demby, S.M.Ferranti & M. Santos (2005), 'Doing Prison Research: Views from Inside', *Qualitative Inquiry*, 11 (2): 249–264.

Bourdieu, P. (1997). 'Verstehen', in Bourdieu, P. (ed.), *Das Elend der Welt: Zeugnisse und Diagnosen alltäglichen Leidens an der Gesellschaft*, 779–822. Konstanz: UVK Universitätsverlag Konstanz.

Bundesamt für Statistik (2007), *Erhebung zum Freiheitsentzug. Untersuchungshaft:*

Unterschiedliche kantonale Anordnungen. Medienmitteilung vom 27.02.2007. Neuchâtel: Bundesamt für Statistik.

Fleisher, M. (1989), *Warehousing violence.* Newbury Park: Sage.

FOJ (2006), *The penal system in Switzerland: Survey of the structure of the execution of sentences and measures, types of sanctions and penal institutions.* Bern: Federal Office of Justice, Section for the execution of sentences and measures.

Giddens, A. (1984), *The constitution of society: Outline of the theory of structuration.* Cambridge: Polity Press.

Goffman, E. (1961a), 'On the Characteristics of Total Institutions: Staff – Inmate Relations', in Cressey, D. (ed.), *The Prison: Studies in Institutional Organization and Change.* 68–106. New York: Holt, Rinehart and Winston.

Goffman, E. (1961b), 'On the Characteristics of Total Institutions: The Inmate World', in Cressey, D. (Ed.), *The Prison: Studies in Institutional Organization and change.* 15–67. New York: Holt, Rinehart and Winston.

HM Inspectorate of Prisons (2006), *Foreign national prisoners: a thematic review.* London: HM Inspectorate of Prisons.

HM Prison Service (2004), *Information and Advice for Foreign National Prisoners.* London: HM Prison Service, Prison Reform Trust, London Probation.

Jones, R. S. (1995), 'Uncovering the Hidden Social World: Insider Research in Prison', *Journal of Contemporary Criminal Justice*, 11 (2): 106–118.

Le Caisne, L. (2000), *Prison. Une ethnologie en centrale.* Paris: Editions Odile Jacob.

Liebling, A. (1999), 'Doing Research in Prison: Breaking the Silence?' *Theoretical Criminology*, 3 (2): 147–173.

Malinowski, B. (1972), *Argonauts of the Western Pacific: an account of native enterprise and adventure in the Archipelagoes of Melanesian New Guinea.* London: Routledge & Kegan Paul.

Patenaude, A. L. (2004), 'No Promises, But I'm Willing to Listen and Tell What I Hear: Conducting Qualitative research among Prison Inmates and Staff', *The Prison Journal*, 84 (4): 69–91.

Rhodes, L. A. (2001), 'Toward an Anthropology of Prisons', *Annual Review of Anthropology*, 30: 65–83.

Thomas, J. & J. B. Marquart (1987), 'Dirty Knowledge and Clean Conscience: The Dilemmas of Ethnographic Research', in Maines, D. & C. Couch (eds.), *Information, Communication and Social Structure.* 81–96. Springfield, Ill.: Charles C. Thomas.

Tomaševski, K. (1994), *Foreigners in Prison.* Helsinki: European Institute for Crime Prevention and Control.

Van Kalmthout, A., F. Hofstee-van der Meulen & F. Dünkel (eds.) (2007a), *Foreigners in European Prisons: Volume 1.* Nijmegen: Wolf Legal Publisher (WLP).

Van Kalmthout, A., F. Hofstee-van der Meulen & F. Dünkel (eds.) (2007b), *Foreigners in European Prisons: Volume 2.* Nijmegen: Wolf Legal Publishers (WLP).

Wacquant, L. (2002), 'The curious eclipse of prison ethnography in the age of mass incarceration', *Ethnography*, 3 (4): 371–397.

Waldram, J. B. (1998), 'Anthropology in prison: Negotiating consent accountability with a "captured population"', *Human Organization*, 57 (2): 238–244.

Weber, M. (1968), *Economy and society: An outline of interpretive sociology.* New York: Bedminster press.

Wicker, H. (2002), 'Ethnologische Überlegungen zu einem Strafvollzug im Zeitalter zunehmender transnationaler Mobilität', in Baechtold, A. & A. Senn (eds.), *Brennpunkt Strafvollzug – Regards sur la prison.* 223–237. Bern: Stämpfli-Verlag.

PART TWO

Rethinking Basic Research Methods

3

Different Methods to Research Irregular Migration

RICHARD STARING

Starting in 1993 I have, in divergent ways and in the context of different projects, been doing empirical research on irregular migration processes and undocumented migrants[1] (cf. Burgers & Engbersen 1999, Staring 2001, Engbersen et al. 2002, Staring et al. 2005). Since the beginning of the 1990s, the immigration policies set by the Dutch government have been characterised by an ever-increasing restrictiveness. The possibilities for foreigners to settle in the Netherlands in a legal manner have been reduced and the Dutch government is increasingly trying to deny irregular migrants access to the welfare state by raising internal borders. This context of formal exclusion and marginalization raises the question of how undocumented migrants nevertheless succeed in settling in the Netherlands; and how and to what extent illegally residing migrants have succeeded in integrating in the Netherlands. Underlying these two basic questions are more precise questions that to an important extent refer to theoretical notions of social capital (Bourdieu 1989, Portes 1995) and reciprocity (Mauss 1967, Sahlins 1972). Such research questions cannot be answered on the basis of statistical analyses of large-scale databases. Nor is it possible to form a probability sample of the whole population of irregular migrants and submit this sample to a survey. This is simply because these undocumented immigrants lack a residence permit, are not registered with local authorities, thereby do not exist on paper, and are absent from the databases. Questions about the underlying patterns of support and signification, moreover, imply direct contact with the persons involved; only they can answer to that and motivate their support. On the basis of the idea that the research question dictates the method to be followed and given the limited registrations, it is a matter of making use of different ethnographic research methods, among which there are classical methods such as (in)formal conversations, participation, and observation.

Through ethnographic research among Turks in the Netherlands, I have been able to formulate a detailed answer to the question of how their coming to the Netherlands took shape in the context of immigration-restrictions and family loyalties. However, the world of the more or less professional and organised human smugglers who facilitated the journey of the illegal Turks and others largely remained hidden. Illegal Turks, who had themselves been smuggled into the country against a charge and with the help of criminal organisations, usually proved incapable of providing insights into the commercial social structures that had taken them to the Netherlands. It simply proved impossible to answer questions about the social organisation of human smuggling on the basis of my existing ethnographic research. What research methods can one employ when the central questions are directed toward the nature of the bonds within a criminal organised network, the hierarchical relations (domination) and divisions of tasks (coordination) in such collaborative structures (DiMaggio 2001)? Of course ethnographic research on 'organised crime associations' is not impossible. Zaitch (2002) conducted long term fieldwork amidst Colombian cocaine dealers in the Netherlands. Another arbitrary example is provided by Jankowski (1991) who for more than a decade studied gangs in New York, Los Angeles and Boston. Zhang and Chin (2002) have proved the relevance of ethnography for the study of human smuggling in their publications on 'snakeheads'. Instead, I chose closed judicial investigations in order to gain a clear understanding of the social organisation of human smuggling.[3] Why this choice for this specific source, and how useful are these 'police files' in answering questions on the social structures and nature of the underlying social relations? What does the use of this source that has been screened by the authorities mean for scientific standards such as reliability, external validity, and verifiability? In this contribution, I will first describe the ethnographic research methods I employed, before setting forth the analysis of the judicial investigations. Finally both approaches will be compared side by side by describing their (dis)advantages and their meaning for improving the understanding of human smuggling and its meaning for the participants.

Ethnographic research among irregular migrants

From the beginning of my research on the arrival and incorporation of illegal Turks, it was clear to me that settling among this group would be a precondition for the research's success. For various reasons the research is situated mostly in Rotterdam and from 1993 onward I and my partner moved to live there. My first visit in the summer of 1993 to Rotterdam's *Bloemenhof* (lit. 'Flower Garden') neighbourhood – one of the neighbourhoods that has a reputation for its large number of inhabitants of Turkish background – was both inspiring and gloomy. In a positive sense I particularly remember the massive Turkish activity, shop by shop, a mosque, the many tearooms, and the many migrants in the streets. The melancholy atmosphere was created particularly by the imminent urban renewal, as a result of which it seemed there were more premises boarded up than there were inhabited. Eventually we found a house on the outskirts of *de Oude Noorden* (lit. 'the old North') – one of the nineteenth century urban districts on the outskirts of the city centre, where we coincidentally looked out on a Turkish mosque with a tearoom and a meeting place. This mosque played an important role during the fieldwork.

The move to Rotterdam marked the beginning of a long period of field-work, which in a structural manner but with varying intensity lasted until 2001. I gained some trust among the Turkish migrants in the different research locations thanks to my knowledge of Turkey and the passion I share with many Turks for *Galatasaray, the* soccer club from Istanbul. Also my command of the Turkish language lead to amusing conversations and commanded respect among members of the groups I was researching, who were not used to being addressed by Dutch people in their own language. Moreover, many 'tourists' – *turist is* the emic term by which illegal Turks are denoted by compatriots – hoped to procure something for themselves through their contact with me. Some had the idea that I might be able to help them find a job, others wanted to improve their Dutch or had specific problems for which they could use my support or advice. Where possible I responded to these requests. Thus I accompanied ill tourists to the family doctor and supported them in their attempts to get connected to regular language teaching. I translated official letters, filled in application and invi-tation forms, and wrote pressing letters to the queen with requests for legalization. Part of my clothing and household goods ended up with the tourists and on request of some members of the board of a mosque, I taught Dutch language classes for one year. I played a role in the attempt of a tourist to legalize his stay through a marriage of convenience and brought tourists into contact with lawyers and visited the legal advice centre with them. I did not comply with all forms of support that tourists or their legal compatriots tried to claim. I for instance left the many requests from tourists to find them a wife or a job unanswered. From the immediate vicinity of my home, I informally participated as much as possible in the Turkish community. This meant that I bought my daily groceries mainly in Turkish shops, had my hair cut at a Turkish hairdresser's, had my shoes polished at the shoe shiner's, and went to drink coffee in the tearooms where one could also play a good game of *tavla*, and where I could watch the many directly broadcasted soccer matches. During the fieldwork I kept in close touch with at least fifty-two tourists. The formal interviews with these respondents, the countless informal conversations with them and other Turkish migrants, and my participation in Turkish life in Rotterdam between 1993 and 2001 form the basis of my doctoral thesis (Staring 2001).

In search of Turks without a residence permit

The contacts with illegally resident Turks and the people with whom they go about were initiated in three different ways: the approach via public agencies, the site-oriented approach, and finally the snowball method. These three approaches have been used side by side during the periods of the fieldwork. These strategies are intended to contact potential respondents in order to then obtain relevant information through conversations and interaction with them and through participation in their daily life. Looking back, however, I can see that the route to the undocumented migrant and the mistakes that I made during my search for illegal Turks have in themselves also been of great importance in being able to formulate answers to the research questions.

The approach via public agencies turned out to be the most toilsome strategy of contacting tourists. On the basis of my presupposition that irregular migrants enter into a relationship with public bodies in a number of domains, I approached these agencies with a double aim: in the first place to interpret the subject matter of illegality from the field of the professions, and in the second place to find access to Turks living illegally in the Netherlands. I have spoken with teachers, family doctors, staff members of primary schools, midwifes, and in particular with community workers, who were active in most of the local community centres. As a rule, the community workers concerned were those of Turkish origin who were specifically engaged with the Turks in the neighbourhood and who had in the course of years built up an intimate knowledge of the Turkish community. I therefore invariably ended each interview with a community worker with the question whether they knew irregular migrants and whether they would be willing to bring me into contact with them. Most of the community workers were not willing to do so. Many of them had objections of principle. The contact they maintained with undocumented migrants was based on trust – the community workers reasoned – and they feared their personal relation with the client would become endangered if they would bring me into contact with them. Some of them also claimed not to have the right contacts at their disposal and again others did not see any benefits in it for the irregular migrants. A limited number of community workers, however, was indeed prepared to bring me into contact with the target group. Often, however, this happened in an indirect manner and required passing various 'gatekeepers' before I would eventually be able to shake hands with a tourist.

My acquaintance with the young tourist Kerim forms a striking example of this line of approach via public agencies.[4] One evening one of the helpful community workers introduced me to ten or so animatedly talking, elderly first-generation guest-worker migrants. Everybody listened politely to my story, but at the same time seemed little interested. Eventually I got talking to Ali. He advised me to visit the senior citizens centre the next morning where he would go and play cards. When I arrived the next day, Ali immediately started explaining my presence and stressed that they did not have to fear me: 'He does not work for the police, but is just a researcher who wants to write a book about irregular migrants'. He concluded his succinct argument with the question who knew any undocumented migrants. One of his friends turned out to know an illegally resident nephew – Kerim, at which Ali urged him to call this person right away. To my surprise he indeed took the phone and returned with the message that Kerim would be willing to talk to me and that we were welcome at his house. Together we, at eleven in the morning, rode on line 21 to *Zuid* (South) to return home only in the evening. Various informal encounters with Kerim and his family would follow. Looking back I would say that it would have been difficult to get in touch with Kerim in another way. He had only recently come to the Netherlands and seldom went outside for fear of arrest.

This anecdote first of all shows how their legally resident compatriots screen tourists from the public. As a researcher you do not immediately have access to this world. Without the help of Ali and the confidence his circle of friends had in him, I probably would never have been able to make contact with Kerim. I also remained in contact with Ali and that contact had another interesting sequel for me. After several weeks, to my great surprise, he told me that he was renting rooms to two tourists whom I should definitely get acquainted to some time. The late moment at which Ali made this 'remark' to me, was a first indication to me that the screening of tourists did not take place solely out of loyalty but could also be motivated by the conflict of interest between the established Turks and tourists.

Besides this approach of tourists via public agencies, I conducted research on a number of locations where one could logically expect to find irregular migrants. In the first instance this site-oriented approach focused strongly on charitable institutions such as the *Pauluskerk* (a church in the center of Rotterdam, well-known for the support it offers to rejected asylum seekers as well as drug addicts), *Perron Nul* (lit. Platform Zero), and the Missionaries of Charity. In these and similar locations I certainly encountered a large number of irregular migrants, but only very rarely were they of Turkish origin. Rotterdam's '*gedoogzone*' ('tolerance zone' – an area where certain illegal activities around drugs were officially tolerated) *Perron Nul* , which was closed in 1995, was predominantly intended for drug addicts. From their registration list it indeed turned out that there was a relatively large number of foreigners without residence permits among these drug addicts, but only in a few cases did this concern someone of Turkish origin. I reached a similar conclusion after a few visits to the Missionaries of Charity where homeless people are offered a free hot meal. Also here we did not encounter illegal Turks among the clientele. How should the absence of illegal Turks at regular shelters be interpreted? Did their absence at *Perron Nul* mean that there were no addiction problems among illegal Turks? Should we have concluded that no homeless Turks were staying in Rotterdam? The absence of Turkish tourists at the charitable institutions formed a first indication of the fact that the social world of Turkish tourists was another one to that of irregular migrants from many other countries of origin. Their absence could be explained moreover by the circumstance that Turkish tourists were better off in terms of income and accommodation than undocumented migrants from different countries.

Early on in the fieldwork it became clear that it was necessary to visit other locations to meet Turkish tourists. The Turkish infrastructure with its cultural associations, mosques, tearooms, and other Turkish enterprises therefore almost from the beginning of the fieldwork became the most important research locations. In the first instance I conducted extensive fieldwork in and around a Turkish mosque, to which, apart from a prayer room, also belonged a tearoom, a hairdresser's, and a greengrocer's. I visited this complex daily during a period of several months. The members of the board were informed of my research and had also given permission for it. During the first two years of the fieldwork, I found relatively many respondents in and around this mosque willing to participate in the research. Apart form this mosque, the other most important research locations to the north of the river *Maas* were a Turkish cultural association, a hairdresser's, a tearoom, and a green grocer's. To the south of the *Maas* these were a video shop, two tearooms, and a hairdresser's set up in one of the spaces belonging to a mosque.

Apart from the approach of tourists via public agencies and the site-oriented approach, I constantly tried to get new respondents via the snowball method. The 'snowball method' is a sample-method often used in ethnographic research and is frequently applied in approaching research subjects who are difficult to get access to. In various American studies on 'undocumented migrants' this recruitment method was also successfully employed (see for instance Chavez 1992, Mahler 1995). I asked tourists whom I spoke with to bring me into contact with other tourists, whom I in turn requested to introduce me to again other tourists. Ideally such an approach of respondents follows the social relations of people in a certain context, with the important additional advantage that clarity can also be obtained on the nature of the relations between these persons. The latter is of relevance in a research in which the social network of the research subjects and the support that does (or does not follow from this) are central. The snowball method was applied with varying success and often I could not get the 'snowball' rolling. Some tourists indicated that they did not know of other tourists, what I for that matter found highly implausible. Others did not – despite their familiarity with me – take notice of my request because pointing out illegally resident migrants is unusual also among the circle of migrants themselves (see also Dahinden & Efionayi-Mäder in this book).

A half exception to this rule was formed by Mustafa, a young enthusiastic worker in the garment industry of Rotterdam, who had to my big surprise brought along three friends to an engagement, of whom it turned out they were also staying in the Netherlands without a residence permit. I had agreed to go and talk with Mustafa near 'the Castle' in the neighbourhood *Spangen* about his experiences in the sewing workshops. Surprised by this situation I decided to have a more general talk among the five of us instead. After this conversation I got to talking to one of them – Hassan – and arranged an interview with him a few days later. That particular afternoon Hassan however did not show up. I started doubting my appointment and wondered whether perhaps my Turkish had played tricks on me and had made me get the appointment all wrong. Also the following day, however, I did not get to see or speak to Hassan. People who knew him, however, also had not seen him for some days, which could mean he had been arrested and been deported from the country. Only after several weeks did I stumble across Hassan again in *Spangen* and after some time I asked him about our missed appointment. Hassan told me I had understood the appointment correctly but that he had later changed his mind. He made it clear to me that by showing up at the agreed time and place and talking to me he would have publicly revealed that he was staying in the Netherlands illegally. 'No one except my uncle's family knows that I am illegal, I act as if I am legal, pay taxes, and go around insured. If Turks know that I am illegal they take advantage of that'. The Turks in the center where I had agreed to meet Hassan knew that I was writing a book about illegal Turks and if one of them would see me interviewing Hassan it would also become clear to everyone that Hassan belonged to the category of tourists. In another conversation Hassan adds to this:

> The very worst here is being illegal, the very worst . . . Because they [legal Turks; R.S.] do not talk to you. They treat you like an entirely different person. Nobody says anything to you. Nobody for example knows of me being a tourist. I have not said anything about it to anyone . . . Because you are a tourist, they do not treat you with respect. . . . Here even dogs have more value than tourists.

Hereafter I continued to keep up with Hassan for years and frequently talked to him but this ostensibly peripheral incident – a respondent not keeping his appointment – was more meaningful than all the answers he gave to my questions. His explanation focused my attention more and in a different way than before on the members of the Turkish communities. Till then I was under the impression that the screening of illegal Turks was primarily directed outward, outside the Turkish communities; toward policemen, civil servants, and people like myself of whom they possibly had all sorts of things to fear. This incident however illustrated that tourists had just as much to fear from legally resident compatriots. Besides all the support tourists receive from their networks, the screening off from compatriots was also of great importance in being treated in an equal manner and in not risking being exploited or betrayed.

Criminal investigations of organised human smuggling

On the basis of my ethnographic research among Turks in the Netherlands I have been able to sketch an accurate picture of the manner of their entry, in the context of underlying social capital and other forms of reciprocity. However, the world of the more or less professional and organised human smuggling that facilitated the (sometimes hidden) journeys of illegal Turks and others remained largely out of sight. Illegal Turks, who were smuggled into the Netherlands with the help of criminal organisations and against a charge, usually proved incapable of providing insights into the commercial social structures that had taken them to the Netherlands. Irregular migrants can answer questions on how they came, with which means of transportation they travelled, and whether or not they paid for it, but they do not have insight into the division of labour and hierarchical relations in the network. These questions could be answered by conducting ethnographic fieldwork on the spot, but a research proposal on human smuggling networks in and from Istanbul was rejected by the NWO (the Dutch organisation for scientific research). To answer the questions on the social organisation of human smuggling networks, I eventually made use of a fundamentally different source: judicial investigations in the field of human smuggling. This is a secondary analysis of, to be precise, eleven case files that were collected in the context of judicial investigations. All these files and the networks that act in them are in some way or another connected to the port city of Rotterdam. These are, moreover, investigations that have been conducted in the period 2000–2005.

Before the files can be consulted, it is necessary to obtain permission from the authorities. This permission came after several months against the requirement of anonymity of the persons who figure in the files and of not endangering the potential court procedures through publication. Next, the available investigation reports in the field of human smuggling had to be taken stock of. It turned out not to be an easy task to get hold of an overview of names and locations of the human smuggling investigations since 2000. Government administration did not always turn out to be very accurate and the central administration was incomplete. Moreover, the different investigation reports turned out to be physically present at different locations.

An important third step is developing a checklist. If one uses polices files for a research one cannot start reading the statements, telephone tapping reports, crime reports, judicial documentation, or observation records contained in them at random and just start noting down what strikes you or seems interesting to you as a researcher. What information is relevant, and what is not, is of course determined by the research questions. To be able to gather the necessary data for this from the files in a somewhat structured manner, we developed an instrument – a checklist – that indicates what information should be retrieved. Using a checklist, different researchers can gather material in a similar manner and one prevents that all kind of irrelevant information is studied and noted that does not contribute to answering the research questions. Finally, the information was mostly processed on location in the checklist to eventually be prepared in SPSS and other qualitative analysis programs for closer analysis.

The tracing of (organised) crime such as human smuggling is often reflected in dozens and dozens of orders, full of relevant, but especially non-relevant information. They can form sizeable files in which all kind of material has been included.[5] The files normally contain a 'general procès-verbal' in which the core of the case – in the light of the judicial investigation – has come to a conclusion and that can be seen as a summary of the investigation. In addition to this each investigation contains the original research material – as has been collected by law enforcement officers and others concerned in the course of the investigation. These are observation reports, pictures of the suspects in different contexts, telephone taps either verbatim transcribed or summarised, reports of interrogations of suspects, witness reports, and all sorts of other things one can encounter during the course of an investigation, for instance photocopies of notes, bills, bank statements, or telephone numbers as these have been found in mobile phones.

On the selective character of the material in closed criminal investigations

The material that has been collected in judicial investigations is characterised by selectivity in at least four ways. In the first place there is always a selection on the basis of cases that present themselves to the public prosecutor as 'worthy of investigation'. Cases can be 'shelved' for different reasons, for example because they have insufficient priority at that moment, or because the public prosecutor suspects beforehand that not enough evidence can be collected. Although human smuggling is among the seven top priorities of the fight against organised crime in the Netherlands, the establishment of priorities by the police and judiciary results above all in many drugs investigations (Staring 2006, Van de Bunt

& Kleemans 2000: 269). The second selection moment lies in the circumstance that only those human smuggling networks can be analyzed that catch the judiciary's eye. This perhaps means that only the 'losers' become subjects of study and those successful human smuggling networks that manage to escape attention stay out of range. In the third place, investigation teams may start to concentrate on a specific and limited number of suspects in the course of an investigation. Some suspects may be easier to map or be more interesting to the judicial system than others, due to the nature of their activities. The limited capacity of an investigation team also entails that not all suspects who appear in the course of an investigation can receive equal attention. This brings us to the fourth selection moment regarding human smuggling networks. The attention of the investigation focuses primarily on suspects residing in the Netherlands. Suspects outside of the Netherlands usually do appear in the investigation, but simply run less risk because of their stay abroad. In many cases international judicial cooperation takes place with much difficulty or is even absent.

To conclude, criminal investigations have the primary goal of collecting enough proof against the suspects to be able to arrest and get them sentenced. This line of approach, combined with various selection moments, results in a limited reflection of the actual smuggling network by the police.

On the credibility of data in closed criminal investigations

Sociologist Scott discerns in his 'A Matter of Record' four criteria for the quality of the evidence available for analysis of documentary sources in social research, among which is the criterion of 'credibility'.[6] He defines credibility as 'the extent to which the evidence is undistorted and sincere, free from error and evasion' (1990: 6–7). This credibility of the evidence resembles the concept of 'hardness' as it has been employed by Van de Bunt & Kleemans (2000). These criminologists establish that there are differences in police material in terms of 'hardness'. The 'hardness' of the material in their point of view is greatest in *completed* investigations because there so much evidence has been collected that the public prosecutor ventures to take the case to court (2000: 267–268). Van de Bunt & Kleemans talk in general terms about the 'hardness of evidence-based closed investigations' vis-à-vis the 'softer material' in project proposals or information from the Central Intelligence Service. But it is also possible to speak of internal gradations of 'hardness' of the material *within* a closed investigation. In the context of this 'credibility' of the material it is important to realize that non-scientists have collected the data included in closed investigation reports. Law enforcement officers working for aliens offices or core teams collect data that are primarily aimed at tracking criminal activities and, subsequently, suspects. Obviously suspects are reluctant to give a detailed and intimate view into their network in front of the police. If suspects present insights, this can be to exculpate themselves or place the guilt with others. All suspects and others concerned in other words can have an interest in twisting answers or in keeping mum. A brief look at most investigation reports indeed shows that many interrogations of suspects yield relatively little because they present no or dubious information that can hardly be perceived as credible.

But not all material in investigation reports bears this characteristic. Particularly the literally transcribed telephone taps can yield a wealth of information on the nature of mutual relations in the network and the relations of smugglers to (parts of) their social environment. Important authentic information is implicit in these transcribed telephone taps between members of the network. These telephone conversations reflect daily interactions and this information is not determined or led by police questions. These telephone conversations are sometimes entirely and literally translated and transcribed, and sometimes they are also summarised. By also paying attention in the research to such non-suspect concerned persons, one can get a clearer picture of the structure of human smuggling organisations, their procedure, and their intertwinement with the legal 'straight world'. We mostly mapped out the involvement of non-suspect persons from analysis of interviews with smuggled persons and witnesses, from interrogations of suspects, and from telephone tapping reports. Police interrogations of persons who have been smuggled into the country often describe, sometimes in extensive conversations, whom they had to deal with during their journey to the Netherlands. From reports of telephone taps of suspects, whether or not literally transcribed, it turns out that some are not infrequently called by people who want something from them or are doing something for them, and from the interrogations of suspects names of persons who have in some way or another been of service to the suspect sometimes come up. Concerned family members of smuggled migrants for instance can call smugglers to enquire about the arrival times of their relatives or to inform about the possibilities of having illegally resident relatives smuggled onward. Other migrants illegally residing in the Netherlands emerge in the telephone taps at moments when they are approached by human smugglers with the request whether they can lodge a number of 'friends' (read: smuggled immigrants) in their home for a night. In this manner it becomes clear how closely human smuggling is tied up with and embedded in migrant networks. Thus it is indeed also possible to reconstruct a more extensive and realistic picture of the human smuggling network in which not only (chief) suspects of the police play a role, but also a whole range of other persons contributing, often incidentally and sometimes under pressure, to the continuation of the smuggling process.

Such a precise search in the voluminous police files for all kinds of other persons involved entails a huge investment of time. Moreover, the information we have been able to collect on the other persons involved is for the greater part scant, certainly in comparison to the available information on the suspects. Of some of the other persons involved we for instance have not been able to find more than the report of a tapped phone call to one of the suspects, in which it is announced that the smuggler will be supplied with more clients. After an approving and assenting 'hum' by the suspect, the connection is suddenly broken off. Telephone taps usually provide little information on other persons. The language used says something about the ethnic background of the person and the voice about the person's sex. Sometimes the telephone number of the person shows the location, so that one obtains an indication of the transnational character of the network. In general we can, however, conclude that little information is available on other persons involved, in comparison to the available knowledge on suspects.

In ethnography, triangulation is the best means of increasing the reliability of the data (see also Achermann in this book). In triangulation, the researcher makes use of different sources and examines the information obtained from one source in relations to that obtained from another source. We have also tried to increase the reliability in various ways in the analysis of the investigation reports. First of all by developing a checklist, secondly by performing the analysis in pairs and sometimes threesomes and presenting the outcomes to each other, and, finally, by presenting the outcomes of this analysis to the criminal investigators involved and by confronting these outcomes with the findings from previous empirical research on smuggled migrants.

Conclusion

Research on irregular migration and the incorporation processes of irregular migrants is, because of the hidden nature of the phenomenon under investigation, difficult to conduct via the usual and respected statistical analyses of large-scale databases. Nor is it possible to form a cross sample of undocumented migrants and submit this to a survey-examination. In this contribution two research methods – on-site ethnographic research *and* secondary analysis of closed criminal investigations – have been described. Depending on the specific research question, both methods can be successfully deployed in answering questions on the irregular migration processes and the supporting social capital. It also turned out that it is possible to employ ethnographic research methods on organised crime associations. Using ethnographic methods to study a substantial number of divergent smuggling networks, to thereby be able to interpret the different social structures, would however have been too time-consuming.

Both forms of research come with different forms of selectivity. In the case of ethnographic research, the social skills of the researcher, coincidences, and opportunities that arise play an important role. In order to be as unselective as possible given the characteristics of the research group, I employed several routes towards finding undocumented immigrants from different background and participating in different networks. I, however, looked particularly at the different forms of selectivity for the secondary analysis of information that can be found in closed investigation reports. One could argue that the analyses of investigation reports for scientific purposes merely provide insights in the phenomenon through the eyes of the police, and are unsuitable for scientific analysis. Is this a meaningful argument? The answer to this question heavily depends in the first place, as Van de Bunt and Kleemans (2000) argue, on the kind of research question that is central. Obviously such closed investigation reports cannot provide insight into the magnitude of human smuggling. The selectivity of the material and the blind spots connected to this also, however, need not lead to the conclusion that investigation reports cannot function as a source of knowledge. It is indeed important that the researcher is aware of the different forms of selectivity in relation to the outcomes of his analysis and findings. The selective character of the material also means that the researcher should not trust the 'interpretation of the findings' by the police blindly, but should instead concentrate primarily on the analysis of the available raw and credible material, such as that which for instance lies contained in the literally transcribed telephone taps in the investigation reports. Finally, the researcher will certainly have to account for this selectivity in the eventual research report.

The inadequate access to police material, possibly in particular to investigation reports, poses a problem. The authorities close the investigation reports off and only under certain conditions – which are unclear – are researchers granted access to the files. Investigation reports concern judicial material that is only to a limited extent accessible and thereby also hardly verifiable to academic researchers. At the same time it turns out that a number of investigations used in our particular research on human smuggling have also been analyzed in the context of the 'organised crime monitor' (cd. Kleemans et al. 2002) and have at the same time been used as a source by Soudijn (2006) in his dissertation on Chinese human smuggling (cf. Van de Bunt 2007). Van de Bunt (2007) wonders to what extent the secondary analysis of investigation reports distinguishes itself from ethnographic research in terms of reproducibility, also in the light of the strong personal character of the latter form of research. In my description the important role that chance plays during ethnographic research, moreover, emerges. At the same time I am, however, convinced that other ethnographers who conduct research on irregular migration and incorporation processes with similar research questions and in a similar manner, can come to similar conclusions, be it perhaps through different coincidences and through different persons.

An important difference between ethnographic research and the analysis of closed investigation reports concerns the process of data collection. In ethnographic research, it is the researcher who collects the data. In the second case, others have already collected the data, in this case even for non-scientific purposes. One of the added values of ethnographic research, however, lies precisely in the process of collecting data. The search for irregular migrants made a strong impression on me because it provided insights of what it means for these newcomers to live a shadowed live. Indeed, different crucial 'keys' to understanding the arrival and the stay of Turkish tourists did not emerge from the (in)formal conversations with irregular migrants and asking them questions, but from the search for and interaction with undocumented migrants. If we translate these insights on the importance of the search itself to the case of closed investigation reports, it is evident that that the questions are asked and the collection of data has come to an end. The strength of police investigations lies much more in de richness and credibility of part of the data gathered in the files and the readiness of the material just waiting to be analyzed. Although police investigations primarily reflect the perspective of the police on the topic under study, it is my conviction that a detailed, distanced and critical reconstruction of the collected judicial material can also provide strong and meaningful answers to scientific questions on irregular migration processes.

Acknowledgement

I am indebted to Luise Steur (CEU) for her insightful translation of this chapter.

Notes

1   I use the terms 'undocumented migrant' and 'irregular migrant' as synonyms, referring to those migrants that lack the relevant and valid residence permits of their country of stay.
2   The research has been conducted in cooperation with different MA students in criminal law and criminology, H. Moerland and G. Engbersen (cf. Staring et al. 2005).
3   All names of tourists used in this contribution are pseudonyms.
4   The application of telephone tapping gives some indication of the size of the investigation. In one of the larger investigations for instance, twenty-five tapped telephones were used and during a prolonged period the calls made from and to these telephones were recorded. These twenty-five tapped telephones in that specific research resulted in 32,000 recorded conversations, which had to an important degree been literally transcribed but had sometimes also been summarised by the interpreter.
5   The other criteria are authenticity, representativeness, and meaning (Scott, 1990: 6).

Bibliography

Bourdieu, P. (1989), *Opstellen over smaak, habitus en het veldbegrip.* Gekozen door Dick Pels. Amsterdam: Van Gennip.

Burgers, J. & G. Engbersen (eds.) (1999), *De ongekende stad I: Illegale vreemdelingen in Rotterdam.* Amsterdam: Boom.

Chavez, L. (1993), *Shadowed lives. Undocumented immigrants in SanDiego Country.* Irvine: University of California Press.

DiMaggio, P. (2001), 'Conclusion: The futures of business organization and paradoxes of change', in P. DiMaggio (ed.), *The twenty-first-century firm: Changing economic organization in international perspective*, 210–43. Princeton and Oxford: Princeton University Press.

Engbersen, G., R. Staring, J. van de Leun, J. de Boom, P. van de Heijden & M. Cruijff (2002), *Illegale vreemdelingen in Nederland. Omvang, overkomst en uitzetting.* Rotterdam: RISBO.

Kleemans, E., M.E.I Brienen & H.G. van de Bunt (2002), *Georganiseerde criminaliteit in Nederland: Tweede rapportage op basis van de WODC-monitor.* Den Haag: WODC/Boom Juridische Uitgevers.

Mahler, S. (1995), *American dreaming: Immigrant life on the margins.* Princeton, NJ: Princeton University Press

Mauss, M. (1967), *The gift: Forms and functions of exchange in archaic societies.* New York: W.W. Norton.

Portes, A. (1995), 'Economic sociology and the sociology of immigration. A conceptual overview', in A. Portes (ed.), *The economic sociology of immigration: Essays on networks, ethnicity, and entrepreneurship*, 1–41. New York: Russell Sage Foundation.

Sahlins, M. (1972), *Stone age economics.* London: Tavistock Publications.

Scott, J. (1990), *A matter of record: Documentary sources in social research.* Cambridge: Polity Press.

Soudijn, M.R.J. (2006), *Chinese human smuggling in transit.* The Hague: BJu Legal Publishers.

Staring, R. (2001), *Reizen onder regie: Het migratieproces van illegale Turken in Nederland.* Amsterdam: Het Spinhuis.

Staring, R., G. Engbersen, H. Moerland, N. de Lange, D. Verburg, E. Vermeulen & A. Weltevrede (2005), *De sociale organisatie van mensensmokkel.* Zeist: Uitgeverij Kerckebosch.

Van de Bunt, H.G. (2007), Problemen van transparantie en controleerbaarheid in criminologisch onderzoek, in A. Soeteman & F. vab den Born (ed.) *Ethiek van empirisch sociaal-wetenschappelijk onderzoek.* Amsterdam: KNAW: 27–35.

Van de Bunt, H.G. & E.R. Kleemans (2000), De WODC-monitor georganiseerde Criminaliteit, in H. Moerland & R. Rovers (ed.) *Criminaliteitsanalyse in Nederland.* Den Haag: Elsevier Bedrijfsinformatie: 263–276.

Zhang, S.X. & K-L. Chin (2002), 'Enter the dragon: Inside Chinese human smuggling organizations', *Criminology* 40 (4): 737–67.

Zaitch, D. (2002), 'From Cali to Rotterdam: Perceptions of Colombian cocaine traffickers on the Dutch port', *Crime, Law, and Social Change* 38 (3): 239.

4

Challenges and Strategies in Empirical Fieldwork with Asylum Seekers and Migrant Sex Workers

JANINE DAHINDEN AND DENISE EFIONAYI-MÄDER

Though a lot has been published on migration in general, little has been written about the specific methodological challenges in this research field. This is striking, since many researchers encounter methodological challenges in their work on a daily basis. We hypothesize that there are some specific methodological challenges in studying migrants in precarious situations, such as refugees, undocumented migrants, migrant sex workers or asylum seekers. Though these challenges might not be that different than those raised by other social science research and migration scholars can learn quite a lot from them (see also introduction to this book), they have some specific features requiring specific strategies guaranteeing unbiased data and sound findings. Such obstacles in data collection clearly influence the quality of the data. The aim of this chapter is to discuss three methodological challenges in migration research. The first challenge concerns the access to potential interview partners and motivating them into participation. The second deals with research across different languages and cultural backgrounds, all of which may ultimately impact on the quality of the gathered data. Finally, a third challenge is related to difficulties that may arise when addressing delicate research issues. Our reflections are based on two different studies, which have both been conducted in Switzerland.

The first study, which took place in 2003 and 2004, studied the trajectories and motivations of African refugees and migrants in Switzerland. It was a follow up study of a former survey with similar approaches (Efionayi-Mäder et al. 2001) which allowed developing our methodology further on the basis of 'learned lessons' in the first study.[1] The study focused on developments in asylum and migration policies and their impact on migration processes, as well as on the trajectories and decision-making. A total number of 51 asylum seekers, recognised refugees and a few other migrants (undocumented migrants, students)[2] were interviewed in several Swiss towns. Interviewees mainly originated from West African countries, a smaller group came from Central Africa and all arrived in Switzerland within the last five years. 30 key informants, i.e. community leaders, experts or other persons who are in close contact with African migrants were interviewed as well (Efionayi-Mäder 2005). The planned sample size included more interviews with concerned migrants (80) and less with third persons. The numbers were however adapted in the course of the study for reasons we will discuss later. Interviews were carried out by native Swiss and African researchers and explored living conditions and events before departure, but especially events which took place during the journey and the mechanisms underlying the journey.

The majority of the interviewees were (former) asylum seekers who have experienced asylum hearings by the refugee authorities, which increasingly include conditions and modalities of their travel route to Switzerland. For years most asylum seekers in Switzerland by far have originated from the Balkans, Turkey and the Middle East. It must be noted that for Sub-Saharan Africans it is impossible to immigrate to Switzerland in a legal way, unless they are specialists or employees of international organisations. These were however not included in our sample.

In 2000 immigrants from Africa represented less than 3 percent of the foreign population in Switzerland. Their number has however increased substantially over the last two decades. Many of the African migrants and refugees were (and still are) young men – especially those from West-Africa – from various educational and social backgrounds. They were more subjected to negative stereotypes than asylum seekers. This was aggravated, as a substantial minority of them were involved in drug traf-ficking. As a consequent reaction, many retreated into their own communities, which increased their social isolation and stigmatisation. With this, they also became an easy target for some media who reflected anti-immigrant tendencies. This general context of stigmatization and politicization showed its impact on the due course of the research and forced us to rethink some parts of the methodology. The second study deals with the living and working conditions of cabaret dancers in Switzerland. These migrant sex workers mainly come from non-EU countries. Only very few Swiss women, or women from EU states, work as dancers in cabarets (according to official statistics, 2 percent of the women come from EU states). According to the Swiss Central Aliens Register, in December 2005, cabaret dancers primarily came from Eastern Europe (75%) and Central America (12%), very few from South-America (4%) and Asia (4%). Three quarters of all dancers are cit-izens of four countries: Ukraine, Russia, Rumania and the Dominican Republic. For our research we interviewed 70 cabaret dancers, coming from 11 different countries. We also conducted 30 interviews with experts and key-informants, including representatives of the Swiss administration, cabaret owners and women's organisations (Dahinden and Stants 2006).

The Swiss legislation foresees a special permit explicitly for cabaret dancers from non EU-countries, the L-permit. This short term working permit presents – besides a marriage to a Swiss citizen – the only possibility for women from non EU-countries to legally work in Switzerland if they are not highly qualified. This special work permit, and all the regulations that belong to it, is the result of long political debates on the situation of cabaret dancers. Over the last years, more and more regulations have been issued, and a model contract defines all details of the dancer's working conditions, such as the number of working hours, the nature of the activities and the salary. These regulations have primarily been issued to protect those dancers from exploitation and abuse. In spite of all this, women's organisations and some political stakeholders consider the situation of these dancers as highly problematic. Indeed, one of the main results of the research was that a gap between the official regulations and the everyday working practices of the dancers exists. Although the work of the cabaret dancers is subjected to detailed legal regulations with regard to their stay and their activities in the cabarets, many offer services, which, from a legal point of view, they are not allowed to offer. One such offer is prostitution, or more general sexual-economic relations. Offering these services, on the one hand, allows them to improve their earnings. On the other hand, some women are forced to offer these sexual services by the owners of the cabarets or by clients.

Studying such a sensitive topic of course poses different methodological challenges. First of all we are aware that already by applying the term 'sex work' our political stance towards this phenomenon is reflected. We are convinced that we can only understand the work and living conditions of the dancers by considering them on a theoretical and empirical level as transnational actors with 'agency' (Giddens 1985). The aim of our research was not to investigate the theoretical perspective of 'deviance and criminology', but to highlight the conditions of their work and their strategies in dealing with them (Agustin 2006). Sexual work is still taboo and the dancers often find themselves in a dilemma between exploitation and their own economic interests. In sum, they find themselves in precarious situations and some of them are highly vulnerable. Working in the sex industry is often a stigma *per se* which renders research difficult and may cause 'socially desirable responding' (Meston 1998; Paulhus 2002). Also, the reliability of the stories of migrants involved in illegal activities as prostitution for dancers or working in stigmatised areas can be questioned. This forced us to think carefully about certain methodological challenges.

Methodological challenges

At a first glance, these two studies have very different characteristics and follow different research objectives. Whereas the first involved mainly male migrants and studied the migration routes and decision making processes of migrants, the second enclosed exclusively female migrants and studied their working conditions. Yet, interestingly enough, the methodological challenges that arose during the course of the studies, as well as the strategies adopted to overcome them, were quite similar. In both studies we decided to use a semi-standardised questionnaire and conducted interviews face-to-face. As far as migrants were concerned, written questionnaires were not an option given not only the variety of linguistic and educational backgrounds of the respondents, but also the complexity of the experiences and motivations studied. Furthermore, as we had to rely partially on external interviewers – who had access to the migrants or spoke their own language – unstructured interview techniques were not seriously considered, because it would have been difficult to ensure similar approaches and comparable levels of gathered information. We therefore opted for interviews based on a semi-standardised questionnaire and written guidelines of questionnaire-utilisation, which were discussed during collective or individual interview training.

For the interviews with the African migrants we developed a questionnaire with a majority of open-ended questions, allowing us on the one hand to capture a large variety of migration trajectories and to flexibly add further questions during the interview and on the other hand to avoid that the formulation of pre-defined answers induced errors or biases due to insufficient language competence or different understandings of terms, which had been observed in former studies. We also included a few sets of standardised answers especially when simple replies (e.g. numbers, ranks, preferences, etc.) were expected or when we were able to use categories, which had already been proven relevant in former studies (e.g. reasons for the choice of a destination country). Narrative answers were either categorised afterwards during the analysis or in a sort of 'sum-up-questions' in the questionnaire, which allowed drawing a balance of a longer narrative report during the interview. These 'sum-up-responses' have not only the advantage of later quantification, but may sometimes contribute to clarify the preceding narrative answers or detect misunderstandings. A similar approach was chosen in case of sex workers, though we opted for a slightly higher degree of standardization (more closed-ended rather than open-ended questions), which mainly concerned the concrete living and working conditions. However, also in this study we added open questions for core aspects and for 'delicate' issues. The interviews with key persons and experts followed in both studies a more explorative proceeding and were conducted face-to-face by the main research teams according to an interview guideline.

Recruitment of and access to interviewees

An obstacle we were confronted with in both studies was the reluctance of people to participate. The reasons for that got clearer in the course of the research. The interviews with African migrants started in late summer 2003 when federal parliamentary elections were approaching in Switzerland. In the political debate and in the media, various aspects of the asylum policy were addressed. This was not new, as anti-immigrant sentiments had increasingly influenced public debate for long times in Switzerland. The debates focused on costs of immigration, control, security and asylum seekers as 'criminals and drug dealers'. The success of the anti-immigrant nationalist party (Swiss Peoples Party, SVP) was something new. Also a prominent SVP leader ended up being elected Minister of Justice and Police in December 2003, in which capacity he was in charge of migration and asylum. Though not informed in detail about political developments, many African migrants we approached adopted a defensive attitude, fearing judgements or stigmatisation from the researchers. Some potential informants even assumed that asylum seekers seen in TV documentaries had been trapped into being filmed by the journalists without their prior consent. In this context, the interviewers were sometimes considered as belonging to an official body and therefore prone to collaborate with the authorities like the police.[3] This suspicion was intensified by the fact that our interviews focused on migrants' trajectories; the very same topic asylum applications usually focus on. Besides, this topic is also something compatriots, lawyers or smugglers warned people about, because information on routes, methods could be used against them in their asylum requests. Though most interviewees proved to be ill informed in detail about refugee situations, most of them knew the basics. For instance, many knew that an asylum request can be rejected based on the trajectory or the claimant can be made to return to a 'third safe country'. Wanting to talk about exactly these topics filled some of the possible interviewees with distrust, which had to be overcome before we could carry out interviews under good conditions.

The cabaret dancers, on the other hand, feared the research could make them lose their jobs. During the months before the research started, a public political debate about exploitation of cabaret-dancers regenerated in Switzerland. Due to this debate, some cantons decided to prohibit the special short term working permits for non-European cabaret dancers. The argumentation they used was 'the laws which have been issued to protect the cabaret dancers are not effective and the state should have no part in this kind of exploitation'. They consider the abolition of this special permit a way to stop exploitation.[4] In Switzerland, the conditions for entry into the country and the working conditions in cabarets are set by the federal state. The different cantons are the executive. They are not allowed to loosen the federal regulations, but they are free to apply even more severe laws, as for instance not to issue this short-term working permit.[5] After some cantons chose not to issue the L-permit to women from non-EU countries anymore, some cabarets had to close down. They were not able to recruit enough women from Switzerland or the EU, as the salaries and working conditions in Swiss cabarets are quite bad. Moreover, Swiss women, as well as women from EU countries, have the right to change occupation. This is in contrast with dancers from non-EU countries, whose permits are bound to their occupation in a cabaret. This closing down of cabarets resulted in a reduction of job opportunities for dancers from non-EU countries, and thus in a heightened competition among them. In this line of argument, the dancers feared our research could result in the closure of even more cabarets, depriving them of the possibility to work in Switzerland. This was one of the main reasons why they were reluctant to participate. Some also feared the consequences of an interview on a more personal level. This attitude towards our research mirrors the dilemma in which the women are captured quite well: they are sometimes exploited, but at the same time they earn more money than they could in their own countries, especially when offering illegal services like prostitution. In the following, we will describe the strategies we applied to access the targeted populations, given the constraints we faced.

When snowball sampling fails . . .

African asylum seekers and cabaret dancers are considered to be a 'hidden' or 'hard to reach' population (see introduction to this book). When classical accessing channels like telephone books or postal addresses do not work the so-called snowball method is often used. In snowball sampling, respondents are reached through referrals, i.e. through people they already know, persons out of their personal network. The snowball sampling strategy however also has some known and less known disadvantages. A known disadvantage is that in personal social networks there always is a tendency to homogeneity along ethnicity, gender, age, level of education as well as values and norms. This means that people are primarily in contact with people with similar characteristics (McPherson et al. 2001). 'Snowball samples' therefore tend to be biased, including the more cooperative participants out of one specific cluster of networks and leaving out others. Such a sample will thus mostly include people belonging to one specific network of friends or next of kin (Bloch 1999). When using snowball sampling, researchers are therefore in danger of interviewing only people with similar experiences, whereas other subgroups of the society or networks are not accessed.

We deliberately opted for the snowball sampling, because at first it seemed the only possible way to get access to 'hidden populations', but it turned out that in neither of the research respondents could be reached through snowball sampling. Only six of the 70 cabaret dancers have been contacted through the snowball sampling method, i.e. through the referral of other interviewees. The contacting of asylum seekers through snowball sampling proved to be just as difficult. The main reason was the general lack of trust towards the researchers, as explained above. It became clear that even interviewees, who had overcome their own reluctance and actually confided in the researcher, did not always feel in a position to convince others to participate or even feared being suspected of working with the authorities by their friends or acquaintances. In other words many respondents anticipated negative reactions of their compatriots when they referred the researchers to them. The second reason for the failure of the snowball method was of more 'technical' nature: many interviewees did not know the precise address or even name of acquaintances, as they frequently met in public places. This fact illustrates the high degree of mobility[6] of these groups as well as their specific form of social interaction.

Gatekeepers and the importance of diversification

As snowball sampling did not work we tried another method to access potential interview partners: targeted sampling. This means you cooperate with so called gatekeepers who will contact potential interview partners on their behalf. Ideally, these gatekeepers are persons with a high credibility, because their recommendation of the research must be credible in order to convince potential interview partners to participate. Also, they need to be at the 'centre' of different networks in the researched community in order to bridge different sub clusters of the group. A difficulty of working with gatekeepers concerns the limitations of their contacts. As mentioned before, the stories of those less involved with these gatekeepers are rarely reported (Shaver 2005). Every gatekeeper has access to only one segment of 'her or his' community. In short, the limitation of the contacts of these gatekeepers at the same time sets the boundaries of a sampling through this technique (Dahinden 2005). Thus, relying on only one gatekeeper to form a sample will most probably result in highly biased data. The solution for this problem is diversification of the gatekeepers.

The strategies we applied in our research on cabaret dancers can serve as an illustration for diversifying contact points. Cabaret dancers were not defined by their nationality or ethnicity, but by their activity in a nightclub.

Therefore, we could not determine gatekeepers based exclusively on the criterion of ethnicity. A first category of gatekeepers consisted of nightclub owners. Their advantage is that they have direct access to the dancers. The disadvantage is however obvious. It is in their interest that the image of cabarets remains advantageous. Hence, they will probably not ask dancers who are critical about their work in the cabarets to participate in an interview, they will ask those who are positive towards their work. As a consequence, the findings will be biased towards a more positive image of the work in a cabaret. A second category of gatekeepers consisted of women's organisations. They try to realise better and more rights for cabaret dancers and often offer free legal consultation. They, like the owners, have direct access to the dancers, but the interviews of these dancers might reversely be biased towards a more negative image of the cabarets. These women are most likely to have been confronted with problems in the cabaret, for instance not getting paid the (whole) salary or having been coerced into prostitution by the cabaret owners or clients. A third group of gatekeepers were the local administration. Some local offices organised monthly information sessions for cabaret dancers. We were allowed to assist these sessions and to present our research project. Women who were willing to participate were asked to write down their telephone numbers. Here, the disadvantage was that the dancers sometimes had difficulties distinguishing between the research and the administration.

The strategy of diversifying gatekeepers was also applied in the study among asylum seekers: this group was however defined by their nationality or ethnicity. Therefore, we looked for gatekeepers primarily among migrants' associations. Through a previous study on African migrants' associations from Senegal and Congo, we already knew some potential key informants. They proved to be of rather limited use, because some of the associations from West Africa were either no longer active or simply inexistent. Besides, most of the members of these communities had been living in Switzerland already for a long time. An important gap was observed between 'established' migrants and those who had arrived more recently in Switzerland. To avoid being constantly asked for support by countrymen in more precarious situations and for other reasons, as for instance the fear of being perceived as drug traffickers, the established sometimes deliberately did not want any contact with the newcomers, unless they had known each other already in the country of origin.

Again, these gatekeepers coming from migrant's associations could access only a specific segment of the community, because of their contacts with specific social networks. Therefore, we contacted potential interviewees also through social workers or other persons employed in reception facilities for asylum seekers. In a reception centre in Geneva[7] a Guinean night watchman, who spoke several languages, had gained the trust of quite a few young recently arrived men from Western Africa. He was convinced of the importance of the study and liaised with the researchers. This contact proved to be extremely helpful to convince potential and mostly suspicious participants. In this example, two methods to access a specific population were successfully combined: site selection, which we will discuss in the following section, and the use of a special intermediary. In this study, as well as in other studies among asylum seekers, the help of such gatekeepers proved to be of utmost importance for the mere recruitment of interviewees, as well as the establishment of a trustful setting. It also helped to prevent – at least partially – a sample which was biased towards the better-educated migrants. It is often easier to convince well-educated migrants, as they often have better knowledge of the host country and are more inclined to trust research.

Unfortunately, the snowball method as well as the gatekeeper approach failed when it came to a particular migration pattern. Several interviewed community leaders convincingly pointed out a migration pattern that was related to organised drug networks. These networks enclose especially young, poorly educated and mobile migrants of specific ethnic groups, who have a traditional nomadic background or at least a collective experience as business travellers. According to key informants, these young men are recruited in their country of origin – for example, Côte d'Ivoire, Guinea and Sierra Leone were mentioned – and sent to Europe in order to sell drugs on the streets. Once they had arrived in Switzerland most of them were instructed, by the people who had organised their trip, to file an asylum application. However, though several of our interviewees had admittedly been involved in drug trafficking in Switzerland or elsewhere in Europe, all of them reported that they had been recruited after their arrival and not by traffickers in their country of origin. Thus, it turned out to be impossible to contact anyone who had actually been sent to Europe with the help of criminal networks and who was ready to disclose her or his experience. For our research on the trajectories, this migration pattern would have been particularly interesting, even though most of the community leaders agreed that it was relatively rare. The impossibility to access any migrants concerned, related most probably to the fact that their 'agents' closely control most of them. This made them even more reluctant to participate in an interview than other potential interviewees. Finally, as only few of our interviewers spoke Fulani, Djoula or other idioms, the language was also a barrier, as less educated migrants often did not speak German, French or English.

The site selection strategy

A third strategy to access interviewees is the site selection. This method can be used if the targeted population can be found at an accurately defined site, for instance special accommodation facilities for asylum seekers or nightclubs for dancers (or gathering places for street children as Empez points out in this book). Researchers can go directly to these sites to contact potential interview partners. The preparatory phase of a former research carried out among potential migrants in Albania offers another example. In Tirana, it was quite well known where the potential migrants and the smugglers met. There were several small bars and cafés where smugglers and migrants would meet in order to discuss the cost of the travel, the services provided by the smugglers or the needed documents. In this example, it proved a successful strategy to look for interview partners at these sites (Dahinden 2001). As mentioned earlier, site selection was used in combination with gatekeepers at reception facilities for asylum seekers. But we also tried to use this strategy to contact cabaret dancers. Some of the interviewers went to nightclubs in order to contact the dancers directly. They distributed flyers and a short description of the study to the dancers. The use of the site selection strategy was however of limited success in this study, as the interviewers were sometimes denied access to the nightclubs by the owners. In some other cantons, intercultural mediators working on aids prevention have access to the cabarets. Some of these mediators overtook the task of distributing the flyers among the dancers, as well as the cabaret owners.

Interviewers, translators and questionnaires

How to study people who do not speak the language of the interview team? As long as migrants do not speak the local language, all communication efforts, for instance during an interview, are highly complicated and susceptible for cultural and linguistic misunderstandings which puts into question the quality of the findings of such studies. Both research teams knew, from previous experiences, that the use of interpreters, translated questionnaires and external interviewers implicates not only a lot of time and money, but also asks for a detailed research plan in order to ensure the quality of the research. But it is not only the quality of simultaneous translations or the translation of the questionnaire that matters; the skills of the interviewers are also of vital importance. We maintain that these aspects are generally underestimated and need detailed consideration. In this section, we will therefore discuss these issues in detail.

Recruitment and training of the interviewers

It seemed indispensable in both studies to conduct the interviews in the languages of the targeted population. First of all, many migrants had not lived long enough in Switzerland to master one of the Swiss national languages. Secondly, speaking with asylum seekers about illegal ways of entry into Switzerland, and with cabaret dancers about illegal activities, requires an atmosphere of trust and confidence. Conducting the interviews in the language of origin of the interviewee was believed to contribute to this situation of trust. For both studies, interviewers who spoke the language of the targeted research population were recruited. They needed to follow set procedures to ensure reliable and objective data and as 'access difficulties' were calculated beforehand, the interviewers were expected to help accessing potential interviewees. Furthermore, it was planned to involve the interviewers in the translation of the questionnaires.

Sub-Saharan Africans – and West-African migrants in particular – migrate on a rather limited scale to Switzerland and African diasporas in Switzerland are only scarcely researched. It was therefore difficult to find interviewers with optimal knowledge of the research topic and the terrain. Knowing that some newcomers among the less educated migrants were not fluent in English or French, it was important to seek collaboration with speakers of a few native languages (Fulani, Krio, Manding, Susu, Yoruba, etc.) or pidgin. At the same time, the interviewers needed to have at least basic research skills. The team opted for five interviewers with a migration background from the respective areas and four native Swiss interviewers (including the members of the research team), who had good knowledge of various West African communities. All of the interviewers had research experience, but training was necessary to get them acquainted with the questionnaire and the specific topic of the research. The team consisted of four women and five men. In the end, the majority of the respondents – as of the basic population – were male. The number and 'successes' of the interviews varied considerably, which we will discuss in the following section about gatekeepers.

With regard to the research on cabaret dancers, requirements for the interviewers were not only linguistic proficiency in one of the Swiss national languages (German, French or Italian) and one of the languages of the targeted groups, but also the ability to access these communities. Furthermore, knowledge of interview techniques was also required. An advertisement was sent to different university institutes as well as women's organisations on national level. In this advertisement we specified that we were looking specifically for female interviewers, fluent and literate in one of the Swiss national languages, as well as in Russian, Rumanian or Spanish. These languages were chosen because the majority of the cabaret dancers come – as mentioned before – from Eastern Europe and Latin America. We decided to look only for female interviewers based on the assumption that the cabaret dancers would speak more easily and openly about their problems with a person from the same sex. Talking about for instance sexual violence implies feelings of intimacy or shame, which presumably can be generated more easily when talking to someone of the same sex.[8]

Only later, during the actual selection procedure of the interviewers, did we realize the requirements we formulated were quite contradictory. Having the capacity to access the sex-industry or being familiar with the sex-milieu and therefore being able to access dancers, almost automatically excluded the criteria of having in-depth knowledge of German, French or Italian next to the language of origin. Furthermore, these women almost never had experience in interview techniques. On the other hand, the 'true' bilingual interviewer had almost no knowledge of the sex-industry. This resulted in two types of interviewers: on the one side, we got applications from academically educated women, of Russian or Rumanian origin, with good linguistic proficiency and knowledge of interview techniques and methodological issues. On the other side, we got applications from women who knew 'the business', such as former dancers who had married a Swiss citizen and were looking for work, women working as mediators in the context of aids-prevention, and so on. These women could guarantee access to dancers and might have a high credibility for dancers, but they had almost no knowledge of interview techniques or other methodological aspects. Moreover, they often had limited knowledge of (one of) the Swiss national languages.

Eventually, we worked with 14 interviewers, consisting of both 'types' of women. During the pre-fieldwork period, the interviewers received training in research methods and especially in how to apply the question-naire. They were also informed about the legal situation of cabaret dancers and equipped with different instruments to facilitate their fieldwork (flyers with information about the research in the different languages, a list of addresses of women's organisations offering help to cabaret dancers in difficulties which could be handed over to the interviewees, and so on).

During the fieldwork, one of the researchers from the SFM contacted the interviewers on a regular basis in order to discuss the interviews. Concretely, each interview has been prepared and discussed in detail, as to guarantee a good quality of the data. By doing this, potential method-ological problems could be detected. Problems the interviewers faced during the fieldwork, such as methodological questions, were also discussed. This constant contact with the interviewers ensured the highest professional and ethical standards were maintained. The contact guaran-teed that the interviewers were closely accompanied and could – in an atmosphere of trust – discuss ethical questions, which arose out of the interviews. On the other side the researchers could be sure that privacy and confidentiality as well as human dignity were part of the interviews. This was especially important, given the sensitive nature of the research and the potential vulnerability of some of the research participants. If an interview did not meet these standards, it was once more discussed with the interviewer, but not used for data analysis (5 interviews were sorted out because of these reasons). The main problem during the fieldwork was that this supervision and monitoring of the interviewers was much more time consuming than anticipated. The researcher in question was occupied during three months solely with the supervision of and discussion with the interviewers.

Interviewers as gatekeepers

In both studies the interviewers were also deployed as gatekeepers. In addition to the fieldwork, the 'co-ethnic' or at least 'co-linguistic' interviewers acted as key informants for the targeted communities and helped to negotiate access to them. However, using co-ethnic interviewers raises issues of objectivity. It is often assumed that being of the same national or ethnic origin, speaking the same language or sharing a similar cultural background as the interviewed person automatically gives the interviewer an 'inside-status' among the concerned community. This assumption is however highly problematic, and has to be questioned. Kusow (2003), a Somali immigrant in the USA, carried out an ethnographic research on Somali immigrants in Canada. He described in an interesting article how he remained an 'outsider' within the Somali immigrant community, whereas at the same time being very much an 'insider'. Kusow describes how he became a kind of 'suspicious insider', especially in discussions pertaining to politically or culturally sensitive issues. As soon as Kusow revealed being a researcher, the nature of the conversion changed. Although speaking critically about Somalia and the Somalis at first, many started to advise him about the proper things to write about the Somali community in Canada as soon as they knew about his research project. More generally stated, co-ethnic interviewers might be torn between their intellectual knowledge and the loyalty to 'their' immigrant community. This might implicitly encourage them to present their subjects in a more positive light.

The risk of covering problems within ethnic communities increases when the studied community is confronted with negative stereotypes, as observed with the young West African men. They are subjected to various negative perceptions related to black people in general and are, or were – at least at the time of the study – often labelled as 'abusers' of the asylum system and drug dealers. In this situation, migrants from a similar ethnic or national background may be tempted to break the negative image of their compatriots or of members of a community who share the same type of experiences (which is called a 'community of experience' in French). A case we were confronted with during our study can illustrate this point: most of the interviews of one specific well-trained Guinean researcher lacked any kind of details about the trajectories and only presented 'socially desirable' information about 'his' interviewees. Although it cannot be entirely excluded that the information in these interviews were (partly) related to the type of migrants he met, we decided to stop collaboration, after discussing the issue with him. We felt he had difficulties studying controversial aspects of the trajectories and more generally any feature that might shed a negative light on migrants he probably felt loyal to and he did not want to 'betray'. This example shows that the insider/outsider distinction is far more complicated than the professional literature suggests.

The research team also worked with an obviously more experienced Rwandan researcher, in whose case the mix of aspects he shared with the interviewees – migration background and related experiences – and aspects that differed him from them – not belonging to the same community – seemed to be very beneficial for a confidential interview atmosphere. However, this researcher, as well as his Swiss colleagues, also faced situations in which it was difficult to establish a constructive exchange with the interviewee. According to their own sayings 'some migrants felt freer to talk to interviewers who had no connection whatsoever with their communities, others even had a clear positive opinion of Swiss researchers'. Based on this study, it can be stated there is no general rule when it comes to the ethnic or national background of the interviewer, apart from the fact that common languages and reference points can of course be useful.

Another problem arises from the fact that the defined 'communities'- in terms of ethnicity or nationality – are never homogenous, but often characterised by internal segregation or diffractions along social roles and status, such as gender, social class, political conviction, migrant status and so on. In this sense, a co-ethnic interviewer can never represent the 'whole' community and will thus never be accepted by all its members. His functioning as a gatekeeper will therefore always be limited. In case of cabaret dancers, this is blatantly obvious. A Russian interviewer with an academic background will not easily be trusted by or find access to a Russian sex worker. Their lives are too different and role problems are to be expected. In this line of reasoning, an interview setting across ethnic or national barriers may be more complex (language, stereotypes, references), but not fundamentally different from other interview situations. In any situation, professional expertise, soft skills and empathy of researchers prove to be most relevant elements of success.

Translations and questionnaires

In both studies, the survey instrument consisted mainly of semi-standardised questionnaires. Some open questions provided more information about some important or idiosyncratic issues. It was clearly outlined in the research design that the questionnaire would be translated into the languages of the interviewers. However, translating questionnaires into different languages is far from being an easy task. For a study to meet the scientific requirements, each respondent should be asked the same question in the same way, in all languages. One of the major problems with cross-linguistic research is to ensure that the questions are comparable across different linguistic groups and that interpretations are not affected by cultural bias. Bloch (1999, 2004) describes how she adopted two techniques simultaneously in order to ensure the translations conveyed the same meaning. The first strategy is called 'translating decentralizing procedure' (Brislin et al. 1973). Both the source and the target language are open to modification. The second strategy is called 'back translation' in which two bilinguals are employed, one translating from the source to the target language and the second blindly translating back from the target to the source language in order to detect differences between the original and the (back) translation in the source language.

We adopted a similar procedure in both studies. First of all, we produced a German version of the questionnaire, which was tested with cabaret dancers speaking either German or English. Apart from language the pre-test revealed a few problematic aspects of the questionnaire that were very important. For instance, if the women were directly asked if they were involved in prostitution, the answer was always 'no'. They did not consider themselves as having the status of a 'prostitute'. However, if they were asked whether they were involved in 'sexual relations with the clients of the nightclubs', they answered more openly. It was then possible to discuss these sexual relations. Bilingual persons translated the first tested version of the questionnaire in their respective languages (French, Russian, Rumanian and Spanish). A second bilingual person then compared the translations to the German version. This person was asked to indicate all text which, according to him/her, could be translated better or more 'culturally sensible'. The two translators then discussed these differences and decided, from case to case, which translation to adopt. Sometimes, the feedback of the translators resulted in a modification of the German version. At the end the interviewers were actively involved in identifying sensitive subjects or mistranslations. Every single question was discussed within the interview team. The interviewers used their Russian, Rumanian and Spanish questionnaire and the research team worked with the German or French version. Not the literal translation was essential, but the meaning of the question. Every question was scrutinised and if necessary, changes were made to the translated and/or the German questionnaire. In some cases, the literal translations differed, but the meaning remained the same.

Raising delicate research issues

Both studies dealt with socially, morally and legally sensitive research issues. Both interviewees may have entered the country illegally or been involved in earning 'extra money' in an illegal way. However, many of the migrants did not always know – at least in the first place – that they would get involved in such illegal actions. In some cases, interviewees only realised upon arrival in the host country how precarious the possibilities for a legalisation of their stay or a professional activity were. In other words they were encouraged either by kinsmen, employers or smugglers to deceive the authorities, e.g. by hiding or changing their identity, their trajectory or forbidden activities (prostitution). This background placed both target groups in a position where they constantly had to – or believed they had to – present their own history in a way to avoid sanctions with potentially far-reaching consequences (expulsion, withdrawal of work permit etc.). In fact, many of the respondents proved to be *poorly informed* about the host country or the functioning of the asylum system. This goes for cabaret dancers in Switzerland as well. Especially first time dancers often had little knowledge of their rights and duties. Asking them about their working conditions meant addressing a 'delicate' topic. The situation gets even more complicated when dancers are in situations of exploitation. Women have been observed to minimize their situation in order not define themselves as 'victims of exploitation' (Kelly 2002). Anyway, asking this kind of questions during interviews needs a basis of trust and highlights the problems in interpreting data out of this kind of interviews.

The fact that most interviewees felt unwanted or stigmatised in the residence country induced additional pressure on the migrants to present a favourable portrait of themselves and their community. In the study on African trajectories, several respondents told us they had been surprised about *the stereotypes and prejudices* they were confronted with as refugees, as Africans, as Muslims, etc. Therefore, they felt constantly incited to give a positive impression of themselves and their communities. Again, the situation of the cabaret dancers showed some similarities. It was striking for instance they never used the term 'prostitute' to describe themselves. They tried to construct a more positive image: that of a dancer, who sometimes offers sexual favours to friends in exchange for gifts and (money) presents. In case of asylum seekers more than an issue of social desirable answering is at stake. Their stay in the host country not only depends on their actual migration history, but also on the way they are able to communicate with the refugee desk and other relevant actors (NGOs, lawyers, etc.). This particular context places a great relevance on their *self-portrayal* and the way they are able to handle this issue in order to increase the chance of being accepted as a refugee, or at least of getting a residence permit on humanitarian grounds.⁹ Frequently, smugglers or acquaintances also advise on the 'best way' to present asylum cases (Efionayi-Mäder et al. 2005). Consequently, many of our interviewees presented an 'arranged' version of their trajectories (see also Bilger & van Liempt in this book). While some of the respondents distinguished clearly between the version they used to tell the authorities and the 'reality', others got confused about details and over time started to mix up the 'official' and 'unofficial' report of their trajectory. Very often, the established confidence was challenged when the interviewers asked specifications about the trip, because this reminded the respondents of the refugee interview by the refugee authorities.

Different strategies to overcome such difficulties were deployed. Often it was helpful to state once again that our research was absolutely independent of the asylum application and that we understood the fact that some had used another version for the official application. As an example, we assured respondents that we perfectly understood why they had to tell the authorities that they arrived by boat, though we guessed that they actually had come by plane to a neighbouring country of Switzerland and that there was nothing wrong with that. In other cases, the experiences seemed so painful that we decided to skip details, which were not indispensable for a global understanding of the migration process. Interestingly respondents sometimes opened up more easily when they understood that we accepted their reluctance to disclose all the details of their trip; some of them who first refused to talk about a stage of their trajectory later returned to it spontaneously. Another 'trivialisation' strategy consisted in reporting details of other trajectories to avoid that migrants had the impression they disclosed an unacceptable or illegal act we had not heard about yet and therefore betrayed other refugees. When the interviewees understood that some of their migration strategies were already known they felt freer to talk about them.

As we experienced throughout both studies, a well informed, empathic and flexible attitude of the interviewers was an important facilitator in this context. It was interesting to discover with how many different and sometimes unpredictable reactions – before and during the interviews – we were confronted. Obviously, it did some of the respondents good to open up to someone who did not judge their testimonies. Others refused to answer some of the questions. This possibility was offered, as we preferred this to an 'official' report of the trajectory. The research team always explained the purpose of the survey fully and honestly and guaranteed total confidentiality.

Conclusion

When conducting research on migrants in precarious situations, such as

Sub-Saharan refugees and migrant sex workers, all sorts of methodological challenges arise. These challenges can influence the quality of the data and lead to biased findings. Different aspects of two studies conducted in Switzerland were discussed in this chapter, one dealing with asylum seekers, the other with cabaret dancers. In both studies, the main difficulty was to find persons willing to participate in the study. As it concerned sensitive topics – such as the involvement in illegal activities – and as the targeted population often faced different forms of negative stereotypes, it was particularly difficult to motivate potential respondents to participate in the studies. This problem was partly overcome by working closely with trusted gatekeepers who were familiar with the targeted population. Though almost indispensable in this kind of research, such a strategy also has its disadvantages. In general, gatekeepers can only access one segment of the studied population which asks for diversifying the profile of gatekeepers as much as possible in order to be able to cover a wide range of different types of respondents. As far as interviewers were concerned a balanced mix of closeness and distance to the interviewees proved to be successful in gaining their trust. In this respect, a similar background of migration as well as a common belonging to a 'visible' minority group was an asset, while shared nationality or ethnicity was sometimes perceived with apprehension. Besides, the use of co-ethnic interviewers – and gatekeepers – can raise problems of objectivity towards the respondents and in the interpretation in results. Researchers need to be aware of these potential difficulties and develop strategies to tackle them. The methodological challenges presented by research on migrants in precarious situations are obviously not unknown to other studies, but they are certainly more pronounced here. In short, migration research may be more complex implicating multifaceted cumulative difficulties in its approaches, but it is not fundamentally different from other research. We do not need to 'invent' new methodologies, but rather improve the critical reflexivity, which anyway should be a consistent part of the daily work of social scientists.

Notes

1   The study consisted of a quantitative approach of the asylum flows, a policy analysis and an interview-based research part; only the last one will be the subject of this chapter.
2   The term 'migrants' will be used in a wide meaning including all interviewees, whether (former) asylum seekers, refugees, students, undocumented migrants or others. We will however also refer to asylum seekers in particular.

3   This assumption reflects the fact that universities in some countries of origin are indeed not always independent from governments.
4   We cannot discuss this in detail in this chapter. Other cantons, which have not abolished the permit, argue these women will work in the sex milieu anyway.

If they are deprived of their official status however, they will be forced to work as undocumented migrants, which render them even more vulnerable.

5   Switzerland is a state with a strong federal system, which confers a high degree of autonomy to its states (cantons). Police, educational system and social aid, to mention only a few examples, belong to the competence of the cantons. Cantons are allowed to make and enforce laws, as long as they are not in conflict with federal regulations. Switzerland is also famous for its so-called executive federalism: Regarding migration or asylum policy, the federal state issues the laws, but the cantons have a large liberty in how they enforce these laws. In this way, one canton can decide not to issue this specific short term permit anymore, as others continue issuing them. All cantons however have to respect the minimal requirements, which have been defined on federal level. Hence, the 26 Swiss cantons often all have their own regulations for specific issues.

6   Cabaret dancers only have contracts in cabarets on a monthly basis. This means they change their place of work every month, thus travelling through all of Switzerland. Though most refugees and migrant students stay in the same canton, they frequently change their apartments or collective place of living for financial or administrative reasons.

7   Geneva presented itself as an interesting study place, as it hosts the largest reception facility for asylum seekers in Switzerland, with a relatively large proportion of Sub-Saharan inhabitants.

8   We had one male interviewer in our team who did interviews with cabaret owners. He tried to find dancers for interviews as well, but was not able to access even one of them. However, he chose not to adopt a site selection strategy, which would mean he would have to go in the nightclubs and speak to dancers directly. To adopt such a strategy and to frequent nightclubs would have made him almost automatically indistinguishable from clients, as there is an almost exclusively male population in these nightclubs. This would result in a difficult form of 'participant observation', which raises another set of methodological questions and will not be discussed here.

9   This holds true whether they actually have to hide something or not. It is worth noting that some respondents were convinced to *deserve* refugee status though their chances were quite limited, while others who were in a much better position did not have that same hope. A man told us that he assumed only notorious political leaders were accepted as refugees in Western countries.

Bibliography

Bloch, A. (1999), 'Carrying out a Survey of Refugees: Some Methodological Considerations and Guidelines', *Journal of Refugee Studies*, 12 (4): 367–383.

Bloch, A. (2004), 'Survey Research with Refugees. A Methodological Perspective', *Policy Studies*, 25 (2): 139–151.

Brennan, D. (2005), 'Methodological Challenges in Research with Trafficked Persons: Tales from the Field', *International Migration*, 43 (1–2): 35–54.

Brislin, R.W., W. Lonner & R.M. Thorndike (1973), *Cross-Cultural Research Methods*. New York: John Wiley & Sons.

Dahinden, J. (2001), 'Kognitive Entscheidungsmuster von potentiellen albanischen Migranten : eine qualitative Beschreibung und Analyse', in Efionayi-Mäder, D., M. Chimienti, J. Dahinden & E. Piguet (eds.), *Asyldestination Europa : Materialienband zur Studie 'Determinanten der Verteilung von Asylgesuchen in Europa*, 235–288. Neuchâtel: Schweizerisches Forum für Migrationsstudien.

Dahinden, J. (2005), *Prishtina – Schlieren. Albanische Migrationsnetzwerke im transnationalen Raum*. Zürich: Seismo.

Dahinden, J. & F. Stants (2006), *Arbeits – und Lebensbedingungen von Cabaret-Tänzerinnen in der Schweiz. Studien SFM 48*. Neuchâtel: Schweizerisches Forum für Migrations – und Bevölkerungsstudien.

Efionayi-Mäder, D., M. Chimienti, J. Dahinden & E. Piguet et al. (2001), *Asyldestination Europa : eine Geographie der Asylbewegungen*. Zürich: Seismo.

Efionayi-Mäder, D., J. Moret & M. Pecoraro (2005), *Trajectoires d'asile africaines. Déterminants des migrations d'Afrique occidentale vers la Suisse. SFM-Rapport de recherche 38A*. Neuchâtel: Forum Suisse pour l'étude des migrations et de la population.

Jacobsen, K. & L.B. Landau (2003), 'The Dual Imperative in Refugee Research: Some Methodological and Ethical Considerations in Social Science Research on Forced Migration', *Disasters*, 27 (3): 185–206.

Kelly, E. (2002), *Journeys of jeopardy: a review of research on trafficking in women and children in Europe*. Geneva: IOM.

Kreitzner, L. (2000), 'Reflections on Research among Liberian Refugees', *Forced Migration Review*, 8: 15.

Kusow, A.M. (2003), 'Beyond Indigenous Authenticity: Reflections on the Insider/Outsider Debate in Immigration Research', *Symbolic Interaction*, 26 (4): 591–599.

Laczko, F. (2005), 'Data and Research on Human Trafficking', *International Migration*, 43 (12): 5–16.

McPherson, M., L.Smith-Lovin & J.M Cook (2001), 'Birds of a Feather: Homophily in Social Networks', *Annual Review of Sociology*, 27: 415–444.

Meston, C.M., J.R. Heiman, P.D,Trapnell & D.L Paulhus (1998), 'Socially desirable responding and sexuality self-reports', *Journal of Sex Research*, 35 (2): 148–157.

Paulhus, D.L. (2002), 'Social Desirable Responding: The Evolution of a Construct', in Braun, H.I., D.N. Jackson & D.E. Wiley (eds.), *The role of constructs in psychological and educational measurement*, 49–69. Mahwah New Jersey: Erlbaum.

Shaver, F.M (2005), 'Sex Work Research. Methodological and Ethical Challenges', *Journal of Interpersonal Violence*, 20 (3): 296–319.

Van de Bunt, H.G. (2007), Problemen van transparantie en controleerbaarheid in criminologisch onderzoek, in: A. Soeteman & F. van den Born (ed.), *Ethiek van empirisch sociaal-wetenschappelijk onderzoek*. Amsterdam: KNAW: 27–35.

Van de Bunt, H.G & E.R. Kleemans (2000), De WODC-monitor georganiseerde Criminaliteit, in: H. Moerland & R. Rovers (ed.), *Criminaliteitsanalyse in Nederland*. Den Haag: Elsevier Bedrijfsinformatie: 263–276.

5

Methodological and Ethical Dilemmas in Research among Smuggled Migrants

VERONIKA BILGER AND ILSE VAN LIEMPT

In the following contribution we will point out some of the ethical and methodological concerns we faced while conducting fieldwork for an international research project on types, origins and dynamics in human smuggling processes.[1] To get a better description and explanation of types, origins and dynamics of human smuggling and trafficking in migrants, the research design entailed three compatible research approaches, namely document analysis, expert interviews, and qualitative interviews with persons who had themselves been smuggled. The basic idea behind the decision to apply these approaches was to get an overall picture of the entire smuggling process, its causes and dynamics. Human smuggling and 'illegal migration' have become major topics in public and political discourse while the literature that was available when we started this research (2002) only offered two discourses, the economic (Salt & Stein, 1997) and the criminal (Chin, 1999, Schloenhardt, 2001). In addition only few pieces of work, mostly country based case studies, concentrate on the policy and legal aspects of undocumented migration or the social conditions of undocumented immigrants in the receiving society. Thus the picture of the actual process of human smuggling was incomplete.

The scarce data available on human smuggling focuses primarily on the offenders and their modus operandi whereas information is particularly scarce on individuals who had been smuggled. Migrant's accounts are rarely featured as a valuable source of knowledge about smuggling. We were convinced that smuggled migrants can provide insights into human smuggling processes that cannot be provided by any other source of information. Besides, the way persons involved talk about their own experiences might reveal interesting discrepancies in regard to pictures portrayed in public discourse (see also Cornelius 1982). Therefore, we decided not to restrict ourselves to document analysis (such as police and court files) and expert interviews in order to gain insight into the modes of operandi of smugglers and the role human smugglers play in migration processes. As migrants take an active part in human smuggling processes, the inclusion of their narrations was considered to be the most promising way of actually exploring the perspective from within and to gain the depth and quality of information needed to provide a realistic picture of the entire human smuggling process, its causes and dynamics. But let us start where it all began.

For a considerable period of time the research project on human smuggling we envisaged did not find support or funding. The principle problem was seen in our approach to carry out qualitative interviews with migrants who had been smuggled. The main reason for this hesitation was serious doubts whether conducting interviews would be suited to establish accurate and sufficient information on the characteristics of an 'illegal' business such as human smuggling. Smuggled migrants were assumed to be incapable of providing insights into the social organisation of human smugglers and smuggling organisations who had taken them to Europe. In addition, even if persons involved in smuggling processes could provide information, it was doubted that they would speak out openly about such a sensitive topic. Nevertheless, we were convinced that conducting qualitative interviews would be a promising way of providing an in-depth look into the process of human smuggling. By exploring respondents' practical knowledge, and the decisions and assessments they themselves had made during the smuggling processes we would be able to nuance the stereotypical image of 'the smuggler' and 'the smuggled migrant' and to understand their roles in irregular migration processes.

Our aim to include perspectives from within was not appreciated. In fact to our understanding this was a crucial issue as we did not see any good answer to the argument why persons who had experienced human smuggling processes should either not know or not provide information on exactly what they had experienced. Professional review boards or the research community were thus in the powerful position to set the terms for selecting the appropriate methodological approach in that they were not willing to questions their beliefs over the production of knowledge in this specific area. By doing so they also decided over what type of information would benefit society and what would not, on who has a say and who has not. We finally succeeded with insisting on our position that also in regard to this research topic, beliefs of persons actually involved in smuggling processes should not only be reproduced from outside the context but, in our research, voices and perspectives from within should be admitted and incorporated. Still, over this period of negotiation we had to realise that even before starting the research basic ethical questions had emerged which were not connected to the research design, process or distribution of results and therefore were beyond the control of the researcher.

It is clear that from a methodological point of view the perspectives of marginalised and vulnerable persons, which these migrants are, are 'problematic'. As we show, they may be subject to several constraints. Conducting and analysing the interviews, once we had obtained the funding, proved to be the most challenging part in the course of the project. This article points out that, apart from an often traumatic experience, external structural factors such as the respective migration and integration policy framework but also smugglers or the migrant community itself have an impact on how participants present and represent themselves and their migration process. In addition, due to the very nature of human smuggling processes of touching upon 'illegal' or semi-legal activities, research involving smuggled persons raises a number of delicate methodological questions. We had to ask to what extent and in which way the fact of irregularity in migration processes is likely to influence individual biographies and narrations and how to deal with the findings of our research in an ethical way (see also Bilger & van Liempt 2006).

Data available on human smuggling

When investigating on available data sources that might be useful to understand human smuggling processes, it was understood that information is scarce. Databases, which could theoretically serve as an information tool in this regard, usually contain useful administrative data based on legal regulations such as Alien and Asylum legislation or Criminal Law. In regard to human smuggling, these data collections focus primarily on the offenders (smugglers) and their modus operandi, whereas information on smuggled individuals is extremely scarce. As many asylum seekers had been smuggled at some time in their migration process, we looked at asylum application interviews or protocols of asylum hearings as a possible source of information. However, as the purpose of these interviews is to decide on whether a person qualifies for a refugee as defined in the 1951 Geneva Refugee Convention, data collected by asylum authorities mainly contains information on the reasons to seek asylum and the motives to leave a country. Some attention is however also paid to modes of travel and routes taken, but this data is less detailed. Still, if such data is at all accessible, the major problem when using these data for researching individuals' migration processes is the setting in which information is provided. The process on how this information is collected has an effect on the quality and reliability of these data. The applied techniques of interrogation are *inter alia* targeted to find inconsistencies within flight biographies. An example of this kind of pressure asylum seekers may experience and its possible consequences was provided by an Iraqi woman who was interviewed in the Netherlands:

> I had the feeling they wanted me to make the story simpler than it was. I

constantly had the feeling I was forgetting important details. And the most horrible thing was when I talked about painful events they did not want to know how it must have been for me. They said they had enough information now. They did not even comfort me.

While this example shows that such kind of interviews favours especially those able to express themselves in a clear way, it also shows that interviewed persons fear not providing the 'right' information and therefore lacking substantial ground for asylum. As the applicants' narrations will be used for a negative or positive decision on their application for asylum, this might easily lead to concealment of details or to 'adjustments' in narrated flight biographies from the respondents' side.

Another often revealed example was the negative experience people had with translators translating their flight stories to the authorities. Some of our interview partners emphasised that now, as they spoke some Dutch or German, they were shocked about how their interviews had been translated. Issues that were of real importance to them were translated as if they were minor details while other things were blown up out of proportion so that they themselves sensed that they had lost control over presenting and interpreting their own lives (see also Doornbos, 2003). In order to get an insight in flight stories not produced under such pressure we decided to look at narrations collected by civil society organisations assisting or accommodating asylum seekers. Regardless the fact that these interviews were most probably conducted in a less interrogative way they were nevertheless also collected mainly for administrative purposes even if not for the public authorities but for the organisations' own purposes. Hence, also these documentations were thus incomplete in respect to our research question. Besides, organisations contacted emphasised that, as asylum seekers might not easily be clear over the role of these organisations (whether they are part of the asylum system or not), and, in their aim to receive asylum, may be unclear in what to talk about and what not to talk about.

After reviewing these data sources and respective data available we were even more encouraged to conduct interviews ourselves in order to gain insight into the phenomenon of human smuggling. But it was clear that the issues addressed above would also affect our work. Why would an asylum seeker talk less attentively and carefully to a researcher than with an immigration officer, a translator or any other 'public' person?

How to build up trust in a context of mistrust?

A prerequisite for every successful qualitative interview is the building up of a trustful relationship between interviewer and narrator. 'Trust' is of special importance when researching a sensitive topic such as human smuggling. At the same time building up trust between both is considered to be one of the main difficulties. For a number of reasons, persons engaged might not be willing to talk about their past experiences or current situation with an unknown person like a researcher, who, if not an insider, can hardly relate to the narrators' experiences. Throughout the research process it became evident that for our respondents, who all had to either flee from dangerous situations or otherwise migrated irregularly, trust and mistrust represented decisive factors accompanying them through the whole migration process, from the time before departure until the time of arranging for a life at the point of arrival. Therefore trust and mistrust have a significance that is only hard to compare to standards an 'outsider' interviewer is usually acquainted with. As a consequence anyone who asks questions about their lives and more specifically about their migration process may be approached with suspicion and great reluctance in sharing certain crucial information.

In order to carry out a successful irregular migration process a migrant depends on trusting various agents, be it travel facilitators, passport brokers or other brokers. As the smuggling process is dangerous in many ways, a person is forced to trust various agents when being 'en route'. In a continuous balancing act they time and again have to decide whether to trust a person or not and sometimes even find themselves fully at the mercy of strangers (e.g. co-travellers, accommodating persons, border officials, smugglers etc.). Thus, trust and mistrust are key factors in the survival strategy and can actually decide between life and death. However 'mistrust' and 'suspicion' do not only play an important role with regard to the migrants but to all actors involved. Migrants themselves are also mistrusted and often intensively questioned from many sides (Hynes 2003). 'En route', acute mutual mistrust between the smuggling agents and their clients is a widely observed phenomenon. As smugglers work on profit basis, secrecy is a very important tool in order to keep 'control' over their clients (Bilger et al. 2006). Migrants might therefore be insistently instructed by their smugglers not to disclose any details on identities or the route and travel procedure. Upon arrival, asylum hearings or restrictive regulations create a culture of suspicion that makes the migrants generally mistrustful again while being continuously mistrusted and intensively questioned from many sides themselves (see also Hynes 2003). Furthermore, migrants often find themselves isolated, discriminated and excluded from the society in the country of arrival and subsequently they mistrust their environment. Researchers are not exempted. On the contrary, already the term 'research' in itself might be something that raises suspicion among interview partners (see also Smith 2002). Although it is crucial to understand why and how individuals develop mistrust towards certain groups of persons or specific situations unfortunately this fact is often not taken into account while doing research among these specific groups (Hynes 2003).

But how do you build up trust if you don't know what your respondents are actually mistrusting? Besides agreed standards of guaranteeing anonymity and confidentiality building up trust requires researchers to understand the situation respondents find themselves in. It also requires researchers to invest a lot of time and to establish personal contacts with possible respondents. Informal settings might help to gain trust as well as the use of open interviews, where respondents feel more comfortable, can talk freely about their experiences and do not feel urged to touch upon topics they do not want to talk about. In our research every effort was made to keep the interview as informal as possible and to have the comparatively long conversation-like interview of 90 to 180 minutes in places atypical to the interview situations respondents had found themselves in previously. A quiet environment was chosen, if possible suggested by narrators them-selves such as in their home or places of accommodation, NGOs, coffee-house, school etc. Interviews were strictly based on the voluntary participation of the respondents and were carried out either with one indi-vidual or in small group settings, consisting of a maximum of 2 or 3 persons, depending on the respective narrators' readiness to talk. Some individuals were interviewed several times when necessary.

The interview method we basically followed was the 'problem-centred' interview which aims 'to gather objective evidence on human behaviour as well as on subjective perceptions and ways of processing social reality' (Witzel 2000: 1) and views interviewees as agents in their decision-making processes and actions in a specific situation. To keep focus, a basic inter-view schedule containing major topics to be touched during the interview was to be applied giving the respondent an opportunity to explore his or her experience with as little encumbrance or interference by the interviewer as possible. In the preparatory phase interviewers were trained to do 'embedded questioning' (Cornelius 1982: 396). Narrators were encour-aged to depict whatever comes to their minds with regard to the topic of interest. By doing so, the narrators were in a position to stress and high-light selected facts of vital importance from their point of view, portray them accordingly and determine the order in which topics are discussed. From a methodological perspective this turned out to be vital, taking into consideration that many respondents, due to the situation they were currently in, had been exposed to continuous and sometimes intimidating questioning by administrative bodies, the police, the asylum authorities, medical doctors etc. and consequently might simply be tired of talking about themselves or might be induced to share their experiences only when they have a notion of being in control over their own definitions of the self and their current situation. In addition most interviews were carried out in the respondent's first language. The written or taped records (for privacy reasons it was not possible to record all interviews) were then translated into German, Dutch or English by the research assistants who themselves were all bi- or multilingual.

How to get access to the research population?

In the absence of a clear sampling frame (smuggled migrants are not registered anywhere as such) it was necessary to adopt alternative strategies for locating respondents. Asylum seekers were easy to locate as they are usually accommodated under public care. As such site selection has been a possibility to locate possible respondents (see also Dahinden & Efionayi-Mäder and Empez in this book). But their 'insecure' legal situation may still deter individuals from participating in a research project. Besides, the fresh memory of the official interview may have impacted the interview process considerably. We therefore decided to include those who were *not* in an asylum procedure at the stage of the research. We expected refugees who already had obtained a refugee status, rejected asylum seekers and other smuggled migrants living undocumented to be more open to talk about their experiences with us, but they were also much more difficult to locate.

One way to tackle the problem of inaccessibility is the use of the so-called snowball sampling method. Snowball sampling is a way to facilitate access to respondents where they represent a comparatively small population or where some specific degree of trust is required to initiate the contact. Various studies indicate that snowball sampling can prove to be an economic, efficient and effective attempt in this respect (Atkinson & Flint 2001). In various studies among undocumented migrants in the United States this method was used successfully (Cornelius 1982, Chavez 1992, Mahler 1995). Respondents are obtained through referrals among people who share the same characteristics (Bloch 1999) and 'trust' may be developed as referrals are made by acquaintances or peers rather than other more formal methods of identification. Other authors however, doubt the efficiency of the method as persons are often reluctant to give names and/or contact details of other persons in precarious situations (Staring 2001, Efionayi-Mäder et al. 2001 and Staring and Dahinden & Efionayi-Mäder in this book). Furthermore, the snowball sampling entails the danger of limiting research to a biased sample, since contacts provided by participants themselves will mainly refer to individuals belonging to the same group. Identified characteristics might therefore not be representative for the target group as a whole. To minimize the risk of only referring to the same sort of people it was attempted for our research to establish several different starting points for a 'chain referral' not linked to each other. In our research this method worked out well in cases where no contact details (such as telephone numbers) but only names were to be provided and in locations where possible interview partners where gathering anyway (place of accommodation, meeting places, NGOs etc.).

Accessing the research population through gatekeepers

Gatekeepers typically include persons who are, due to their role in the political, economic or social life, in close contact with the target group on a regular basis and therefore enjoy certain respect among them. In our research respected persons from local NGOs not only managed to arrange contacts between the interviewers and potential narrators, but the fact that contacts were established by someone who was perceived to be trustworthy automatically reduced the amount of mistrust towards the researchers on the respondents' side. Gatekeepers sometimes even encouraged the participation of potential respondents who would not have been willing to be approached without their recommendation (see also Bloch 1999). However also the sample provided by gatekeepers should be critically reviewed. In some cases respondents only participated because they felt obliged to do so and provided information impatiently. This is a typical difficulty researchers are confronted with when including vulnerable migrants in their research, because they need the gatekeeper to pass the gate. Furthermore gatekeepers might choose interview partners they think would fit best and provide information they think the researcher likes to hear. Or they might also pick out respondents who already have a certain experience in interview situations with journalists, researchers, etc., or are very outspoken persons, which of course, may cause distortions in the data collected (Bloch 1999). In order to avoid an 'over-dependence on one network' which might result in the 'danger of interviewing people with similar experiences' (ibid. 372), we involved different gatekeepers from diverse organisations.

Accessing the research population through research assistants as 'insiders'

Another potential source of contacts is the research team itself. For our project researchers worked together with bi- or multilingual interviewers who had personal contacts to potential respondents, friends and relatives who fell under the selection criteria of the target group (migrants who had been smuggled) or who could make direct contact with individuals of the target group. By this the interviewers themselves become 'part of the immigrant kinship-friendship network in the research community' (Cornelius 1982, 387). Some authors argue that working with emotionally close persons and conducting interviews with respondents the interviewer is acquainted which bears several risks such as a biased sample and, as the researcher might be emotionally involved, the risk of 'going native', the over-socialising with the group contacted and therefore loosing the necessary distance and objectivity (König 1966: 37, Bloch 1999). Despite such methodological risks in regard to objectivity the advantages in terms of access and openness were considered more important for our research. Ellis & MacGaffey (1996) point out that when doing research into groups difficult to access and where there is a high degree of suspicion towards the 'outsider' it makes much sense to involve an collaborating 'insider' in order to get access to these networks. The 'insider' must also be part of the network and in possession of extended personal contacts within the researched population. Co-nationals or co-ethnics might find it easier to empathize with the narrator's position and may be more likely to build up trust. This became obvious during the course of our interviews in the form of expressions like '*you know how it is . . .* ', '*as you know we . . .* ', '*you might understand why . . .* ' used by several individuals when talking to co-national or co-ethnic interviewers.

Still, sharing the same ethnic background may also raise suspicion at the respondent's side as such interview situations run the risk of touching upon sensitive political, social or cultural issues of which the interviewer may not be aware. One example to quote from our research was an interview situation with a small group setting of male respondents, all originating from Afghanistan, but with various ethnic backgrounds different from that of the interviewer assistant. This not only resulted in some respondents completely refusing to talk, but also ended up in abrasive stereotypical judgments on both sides. On the other hand problems may also arise when interviewers and narrators share the *same* ethnical background. It might be exactly the 'outside' position of the researcher that induces the narrator to speak more freely about certain aspects, which are usually not easily discussed among the own community. The position of an 'outsider' might also prove to be an advantage in situations where a certain suspicion against co-nationals or co-ethnics is to be expected. In our research a West African woman, for example, was not willing to talk with the co-ethnic interviewer, since she worried that sharing her experiences would be seen as betrayal and information revealed would be spread in her own community.

All interviewers were carefully prepared to deal with possibly emerging problems of bias and confidentiality. Self-reflection and reflections of the general interview atmosphere were of specific importance. Furthermore all interviews carried out were re-discussed and questioned with the person analysing the interview in order to avoid misinterpretations. Indeed several times it turned out that some aspects were taken for granted by the interviewing person who therefore did not ask for interpretation. In such cases it was very useful to have the possibility to come back to the persons interviewed and ask for clarification.

Why did smuggled migrants participate in our research?

It was assumed that a great number of interview partners would not or not easily speak about their experiences in their migration process in detail due to their vulnerable position. Surprisingly, persons did not refuse because he or she did not want to talk about the human smuggling process as such. The decision not to participate was rather related to the fact that these persons had been questioned many times already on their migration process and that they were tired of talking about it again. This was especially the case by persons we had contacted through organisations or other gatekeepers. Indeed, in line with the above mentioned difficulties in regard to contacts chosen by gatekeepers, in our research some potential partners had been approached for the third or fourth time already either by journalists or by researchers. Reduced to research subjects they were just tired of speaking about their migration history over and over again. This hesitation was supported by the fact that during the time of our fieldwork (May 2003–May 2004) 'asylum' was highly politicised both in Austria as well as in the Netherlands, as more restrictive legal changes were under preparation. This discursive atmosphere discouraged some persons to participate, as they knew research would not change anything in their situation and, in case personal information was revealed, they might rather be marginalised even further.

Still, more than hundred men, women and families who had been in contact with smugglers at some time during their migration process actually had an interest in talking about their smuggling experiences with us. In the aim to better understand narration strategies the question on why persons actually *had* decided to participate was of specific importance. It was assumed that specific expectations towards the participation in terms of benefits might be reflected in the respective narration streams. To understand these expectations was considered vital in order to detect certain biases in the narration strategy which could then explain why certain aspects might have been specifically amplified while others were not touched upon.

Asked about their participation, the answers provided by participants were manifold. Whereas for some persons the tense political climate at the time of conducting interviews deterred their participation for others it was exactly this very climate that encouraged them to participate. Participation was envisaged by arguing that they would like to bring their story to public (through research or journalism) so that the wider public would know about what was actually going on in the country. In these cases the narrating person would try his/her best to present the migration process in such a way that the goal of getting attention to their difficult life would be reached best. While some persons had decided to participate for reasons of the presumed scientific relevance of the research for others the interview meant a social event more than anything else. This was especially true for participants who felt lonely and liked to chat about their lives. Many respondents also expressed their surprise that an 'outsider' was interested in their situation and interestingly, simply showing interest in their biographies turned out to be the most contrasting aspect to the official interviews these persons had gone through. In addition, as networking and making friends can be essential for survival when being in a precarious situation other narrations were likely to be amplified by strategies of self-promotion.

The most obvious example in this direction was for example the outspoken desire to be very close friends or even marriage partners to the interviewers. Others again asked for help with legal advice. In these cases the interview was clearly centred on the topics around the asylum system and application or 'illegal' stay. Some people even presented tons of paperwork and correspondence they had with official authorities and asked for opinions on their case.

Researchers in this field must be aware that the relation between the researcher and the respondent even if trustful and close is not equal and clearly influenced by inequalities of rights, legal and economic position, gender and/or psychological position. Sometimes researchers might deliberately be provoked on certain topics to sort out what the possible reactions of the 'native' citizens might be. Like a Liberian young man who played with his 'fake' identity by showing a forged identity card: ' . . . don't you believe me, don't you think I am a British citizen? Why not? It can be possible, isn't it?'

Dealing with information biases in (re)presentations

When certain migrants give accurate information about themselves and their travel process, this might endanger their current position and future options. In migration research this topic of (re)presentation is most prominently discussed in studies on asylum migration. Although extensive empirical evidence shows that refugees conceive an identity which might be very different from that ascribed to them by the institutionalised refugee determination system, surprisingly little is known on *how* refugees present *themselves* within this context. Zetter (1991) raises an interesting point by arguing that refugees may have an interest in the label they are given by others. By recognising that others often categorises them negatively or incorrectly, he argues that it is exactly this labelling that on the other side entails them to certain rights. Presenting one's case in line with what immigration officers expect to hear can thus be beneficial.

These aspects however do not concern refugees or asylum seekers only. Migrants who had moved irregularly, migrants who had used smugglers to migrate and especially those who continue to stay undocumented in the country of destination have good reasons to present and represent themselves in a certain way in order to be able to organise their surviving e.g. in order to find work, get access to health care etc. These conditions influence the way migrants present themselves and may lead to a constant adaptation of narrations according to the requirements imposed on them in a given situation. Often migrants who had moved irregularly and/or asylum seekers not only need to organise biographical aspects in a predetermined way, but consequently have to shift between various representations to which they have to revert. Memory has to shift from 'unofficial' to 'official' identities. Thus smuggled migrants, who run the risk of being interviewed by officials (police, medical doctors, etc.) at any time might be biased in an interview situation and therefore might choose to provide only scarce information or information of only limited use. Most obviously, narrators would highlight certain biographical aspects while other aspects (aspects that might have negative consequences for their lives if openly revealed) might not be touched upon in detail, not at all revealed or adapted accordingly. This demands for an even broader focus by not only analysing *what* is presented and what is *not* presented, but also *how* migrants present themselves and their individual migration process. In order to analyse the collected data it seemed useful to understand more about *why* and *when* our respondents could possibly have kept certain details back or adapted their narratives.

This specific dilemma asks for a very accurate and ethically sound approach from the researchers' side because it could destroy the trust that was built up with respondents. Several interview partners confirmed the need for carefully talking about one's life. The Dublin regulations may serve as a good example of how a certain legal regulation may have an influence on a narrated biography. Without some modifications or secrecy in descriptions on the route or on specific countries a person had transited through the person will not be allowed to stay in the country of arrival, but will be sent back to the 'safe-third-country' he or she passed through. This may explain why often only little or no detailed information is to be found on the final part of the migration trajectory collected by official immigration authorities. As a consequence, explanations on the route may be similar to the following, which was derived from a database containing information on first asylum hearings:

> I came with a direct flight to an unknown place, and then I was brought with
> a white car of an unknown type to an unknown place. I don't know what

countries we passed. I was dropped at an unknown place, somewhere in the Netherlands and now I am here.

Also in our research details on the routes were sometimes kept back but, interestingly, usually for other reasons, just as an Eritrean woman shared her worries with us:

I won't tell you the exact name of the mountain where we were hiding; it is a famous place, you might want to know about it, but there are more people to follow and I do not want to betray them.

At the time of the conversation this woman had no longer been in the asylum procedure so she had no reason to hide information concerning the route in order not to jeopardise her admission procedure but still there were good reasons to hold this information back. Taking into account migrants' social realities helps to place information revealed in context. Still, researchers must also be aware that in the conversation with the researcher the situation of previous interviews participants went through, especially with administrative bodies, may be recalled once more and narrators may have built up a certain expertise in presenting themselves in certain ways. This active use of different presentations of identities and biographical aspects can have severe complications when analysing the data.

There might be information where it becomes clear that the event can not have happened as suggested. 'We were landing with the boat in Milano', as stated by a male respondent from Guinea, can not have happened as stated simply because Milan is not located close to the sea. However, there might also be information where it becomes much more difficult to decide on how to identify such information. There might also be information where for various reasons only some details are simply not clearly remembered by narrators, or from the narrator's point of view are simply not considered relevant. In order to be able to deal this kind of information a first step is to reflect on *why* certain information is or is not provided in this way: did the person just not remember it clearly or confuse the locations with another location he/she transited through? Was he/she instructed by someone to give this answer? Is it the easiest way not to disclose anything that might be difficult to talk about?

In a second step the question then is how this kind of information should be valued and processed: should we just ignore such details of the story? Should we take the whole narration as a 'constructed' story? Should such information just be taken as it was stated or rather should the meaning behind it be questioned? We don't have a clear answer to such questions. However, when analysing the data the researcher has to carefully evaluate information as provided under certain circumstances, with certain intentions or certain expectations, while at the same time reflecting on potential problems which might simply have occurred from misunderstandings and difficulties in the interview situation. In order to be able to interpret provided information thoroughly afterwards, interviewers were thus instructed to reflect critically on their own performance as well as on the specific circumstances of the respective interview in general (duration of the interview, description of the place in which the interview was carried out, general atmosphere, persons present, interruptions and disturbances, impression of emotional state of narrator, impressions in regard to the course of the interview and the interpersonal interaction, obvious particularities in the interview etc.).

With regard to the analysis and evaluation it is furthermore important to be aware of the specific political framework in which smuggled migrants are navigating in order to understand possible narration strategies. Revealing certain details or drawing conclusion without critically reflecting on them not only provides a distorted picture in a bigger context but may also have negative consequences for the participants. Thus researchers should be aware of their power over the distribution of knowledge. This certainly has basic ethical implications and taking them into account is not a straightforward process but a balancing act with difficult choices to be made.

Ethical considerations in the research process

The complexities of researching private lives and placing results in the public arena raise ethical issues which are not easily solved. Qualitative researchers' ethical concerns appear to centre around four major issues: confidentiality and privacy, the assessment of benefit versus harm, informed consent, and duality of roles (Knapik 2002 and introduction to this book). The researcher is in a position to decide on who has access to information, how information will be controlled and disseminated and has the responsibility not to disclose anything that might ease the identification of a respondent. While conducting research on human smuggling the issue of confidentiality and the general rules of guaranteeing anonymity need to be reinforced because failure in safeguarding it can cause serious harm.

The Tri-Council Policy Statement *Ethical Conduct for research Involving Humans* lists three kinds of relationships where the failure in safeguarding confidentiality may cause harm: (1) to the trust relationship between the researcher and the research subject, (2) to other individuals or groups and/or (3) to the reputation of the research community (Interagency Secretariat on Research Ethics 2005). As mentioned above, for several reasons trust is of vital importance when conducting interviews with certain groups of migrants. The consequences of insensitivity in this regard may have far-reaching consequences for the respondents. Still, in our research interview partners set limits on what information they would provide regarding their person. When talking about the country of origin e.g. some would rather generalise or provide us a region rather than a specific country or ethnicity due to the fact that the population from their country of origin or ethnicity was very small in Austria or the Netherlands which may, consequently, make them easily identifiable. Therefore and in the aim to prevent any form of interrogation, in our research we were very much aware of collecting personal information in an open way and only as little as really needed. We did, for example, not ask for the name of the person but had the interview partner choose a name by him/herself. In addition, by collecting this information at the end of an interview, we could not only release interview partners from the need to provide personal information that would potentially allow for identification but also take away tension in this direction and thus ease the start of an interview. In any case, if the trust-relationship could not be established interview partners would hesitate to reveal private details and rather only provide the 'official' part of their biography.

Under point 5 (Rights to confidentiality and anonymity) the Ethical Guidelines for Good Research Practice in the field of forced migration research specifically states that 'privacy and confidentiality present particularly difficult problems given the cultural and legal variations between societies and the various ways in which the real interests or role of the researcher may not fully be realised by some or all of participants or may even become "invisible" over time (. . .)' (RSQ 2007, 165).

For the purpose of our study on dynamics in human smuggling, what is called 'variations of society' and 'locally defined' in the above mentioned statement may be translated to 'institutional and social framework' in which research participants move, present themselves and talk about their lives. The private surrounding for carrying out the relatively long interviews and the individual or small group settings helped to provide the necessary privacy in a safe and suitable atmosphere. Single person settings were considered most appropriate when narrators worried about losing anonymity with others being around. Expressions like: 'don't talk to the others about it!' referred to that kind of fears. Small-group settings proved to be most appropriate with couples, families or groups of friends. In such cases usually one of the narrators would be more outspoken than the others, marking the beginning of the conversation, which made it easier for the others to follow this example. Also for reasons of privacy, in many cases, we decided to not tape-record the conversation. For the same reason in some cases only fragmentary notes were taken during the conversation but minutes taken from memory including these notes were produced immediately after each interview.

In this specific research area of touching upon several levels of irregularities the problem of dealing with anonymity, confidentiality and privacy may however not only concern interview partners but also supporting persons such as gatekeepers or any other person in contact with potential participants. It has to be recognised that insensitive treatment in regard to 'privacy' cannot only harm individuals but a group of persons or a community as a whole. In our study, the fact that failure in safeguarding confidentiality may cause harm to the reputation of the research community became apparent in that insensitive proceeding from the side of the researcher might have consequences for other researcher to follow. Some potential participants, but also gatekeepers, refused to participate by referring to the bad experience they had had with researchers interested in their lives before. We were informed that in this case after the processing of information participants did not find their inputs reflected, to the contrary, research results also referred to by media and policy had, at minimum, cast a poor light on the research participants and their community.

This last aspect is also directly linked to the second above-mentioned ethical rule of 'balancing harms and benefits' where it is the researcher's obligation to strive for 'minimising harm' and 'maximising benefits' with regard to the research subjects. Thus, when doing research on a topic like human smuggling the more sensitive aspect is the striving for minimising harm. Gathered information can quite easily be used by third parties, be it against respondents themselves or any other actors involved. Thus, it should be recognised that researchers and research participants may not always see the harms and benefits of a research project or may not see it in the same way. Hence, this places extra demands for accuracy and sensitivity by which researchers must try to understand the views of the potential or actual research subjects from their point of view. This is of specific importance also in conversation-like interviews as in such settings the researcher is actively working on obtaining very private information.

Thus, the principle of 'informed consent' turns out to be rather complex, as the potential effects of participating are not easily predicted (see also the introduction of this book). Of course participants must have the right to make an informed decision and to hear a full explanation of the research project in order to then decide for participation or against participation. As Glazer (1982) notes participants have their own reasons for wanting to be interviewed and many are able to set limits on what information they provide, also in our research participants had their own reasons to participate and talking about their lives was a vital part of the reality of many participants who had to present themselves repeatedly in certain ways in order to be able to survive or to reach their goals. Still, when it came to more personal aspects and beyond the 'official identity' it became more difficult, just as Cowles notes: 'even those subjects (sic) who appear to be open in their responses to the research activity may become, in the midst of their participation, increasingly hesitant or evasive when they realize that they are revealing information that they would rather not have exposed' (Cowles 1988, 171). Thus, while a lack of respect for the dignity of persons might also be expressed by being overprotective, on the other hand all efforts should be made to provide the necessary space to research participants for presenting their lives in their own way. In this regard applying an unstructured, conversation-like interview style by which interview partners could talk freely and according to their own structure, 'embedded questioning' and the private surrounding in which the interviews took place proved to be very helpful not only in a technical sense.

Another important aspect in this context was the problem of triggering painful memories during an interview and the question on how to deal with the situation when painful biographical events are recalled which, even if unintentionally, open or reopen a hidden psychological wound. In this case the researcher's role becomes even more difficult as the interview can have a profound effect on the narrators' well-being who perhaps had never mentioned these accounts before (Knapik 2002). Also in this regard the open character of the interviews helps to be more flexible in the narration stream as it is left to the narrator on which topics to explore more and which topics to touch less. Malkki (1995) argues that building up trust may in the first place be related to the researcher's willingness to leave some 'stones unturned' and to learn not to ask further when this is not wanted. Research projects where counselling tools were used also taught us that emotional release is greatly helped by a process that starts out as simply taking equal length turns in listening (van den Anker 2006).

The fourth ethical concern mentioned above: 'duality of roles' refers to the relationship between the researcher and respondents and regards a 'balancing of power' and the position respondents are given in the course of a research project (Smythe & Murray 2000). The more active involvement of both researcher and research participants also affects the relationship between researchers and respondents that could be best described as a more collaborative relation exceeding a simple relation of researcher and researched. Although the power structure of researcher and research participants is not equal in many ways the researcher is less influential when it comes to revealing the covered. Besides, in many cases the carefully established trust relation and close relationships developed in the course of a project do not simply cease with the end of the research.

Conclusion

Ethical and professional standards demand for openness to all sides and all types of data and information, and even more so, when it concerns persons subject to the research question. Already before starting our research project we had to experience that these basic ethical considerations were beyond the control of the researchers. For a considerable time the project did not find funding as migrants who had been smuggled were assumed to be incapable of providing insights into the social organisation of human smuggling. Against these doubts, for the particular research project on human smuggling as presented here, it was found that incorporating smuggled migrants' experiences was not only feasible but was considered important for building up knowledge on a topic where sound knowledge is largely missing. Exactly by exploring the knowledge, experiences, evaluations and strategies of persons who had themselves been involved we were able to nuance stereotypical images and common knowledge on smuggling processes, which seemed also reflected in the alleged beliefs over who can provide information and who cannot; who has a say and who has not. Thus, from our point of view the need for more subject-centred approaches in fields where such approaches are less common should be increasingly made possible. Still, realising such an approach entails very particular methodological and ethical considerations and demands specific sensitivity and accuracy. External structural factors such as the participants' specific travel experience, the institutional setting in the framework of migration policy and legislation their particular contact to authorities, their social contacts their responsibilities towards various actors conditioning their lives, have an impact on the course of the project. It regards questions of accessing potential participants, the trust relationship between researcher and participants and the participation itself. At the same time, all these factors also find their translation into a variety of individual strategies to cope with, which are to be considered and dealt with by the researcher when conducting qualitative interviews. A narration may not simply be the story of a life but rather a conscious or unconscious strategy for self-presentation and a legitimisation of projections for the future. We had to ask to what extent and in which way the fact of irregularity in migration processes is likely to influence individual narrations and how to deal with the findings of our research in an ethical way. By researching such a topic a major challenge for the researcher is that s/he requests a certain behaviour from the narrators' side which is not only atypical with regard to the interview situation they previously often found themselves in, also a situation must be created in which narrators have to act contrary to their current survival strategy, namely by revealing private details that can put them at risk.

Note

1   This chapter is based on fieldwork among smuggled migrants in Austria and the Netherlands for an international collaborative project on human smuggling (2002 to 2006) funded by the European Science Foundation (ESF). The main

goals of the research project *Human Smuggling and Trafficking in Migrants: Types, Origins and Dynamics in a Comparative and Interdisciplinary Perspective* with participating research institutions from 6 European countries (Austria, Germany, the Netherlands, Italy, Spain and Switzerland) were to identify contexts of origin, to describe different types and patterns of smuggling organisations and to explain the dynamics of smuggling operations on basis of a common theoretical and analytical framework and gathered specific information for each participating country (through expert interviews, court file analysis and/or interviews with smuggled migrants).

Bibliography

Anker, van den (2006), 'Re-evaluation Counselling as a tool in combating ethnic discrimination and xenophobia', in: van den Anker & Apostolov (eds.), *Educating for Peace and Multiculturalism. A handbook for trainers:* 81–89. The University of Warwick.

Atkinson, R. & J. Flint (2001), 'Accessing Hidden and Hard-to-Reach Populations: Snowball Research Strategies', *Social Research Update*, Issue 33, University of Surrey.

Barsky, R.F. (1994), *Constructing a Productive Other: Discourse theory and the Convention Refugee Hearings.* Amsterdam/Philadelphia: John Benjamins Publishing Company.

Bilger, V. & I. van Liempt (2006), 'Investigacion Sobre la Introduccion Ilegal de Inmigrantes en Los Paises Bajos y Austria: Reflexiones Metodologicas', *Migraciones,* no. 19: 165–185.

Bilger, V., M. Hofmann & M. Jandl (2006), 'Human Smuggling as a Transnational Service Industry', *International Migration,* 44 (4): 59–93.

Bloch, A. (1999), 'Carrying out a survey of refugees: some methodological considerations and guidelines', *Journal of Refugee Studies,* 12 (4): 367–383.

Chavez, L. (1992), *Shadowed lives. Undocumented immigrants in American Society.* Forth Worth, TX: Harcourt Brace Jovanovich College Publishers.

Chin, K.-L (1999), *Smuggled Chinese: Clandestine Immigration to the United States.* Philadelphia: Temple University Press.

Cowles, K. (1988), 'Issues in qualitative research on sensitive topics', in *Western Journal of Nursing Research,* 10: 163–170.

Cornelius, W. (1982), 'Interviewing undocumented migrants: methodological reflections based on fieldwork in Mexico and the US', *International Migration Review,* 16 (2), Special Issue: Theory and Methods in Migration and Ethnic Research: 378–411.

Doornbos, N. (2002), *De papieren asielzoeker. Institutionele communicatie in de asielprocedure.* Nijmegen: Gerard Noodt Instituut.

Efionayi-Mäder , D., M. Chimienti, J. Dahinden & E. Piguet (2001), *Asyldestination Europa. Eine Geographie der Asylbewegungen.* Zurich: Seismo.

Ellis, S. & J. MacGaffey (1996), 'Research on Sub-Saharan Africa's Unrecorded International Trade; Some Methodological and Conceptual Problems', *African Studies Review,* 39 (2): 19–41.

Glazer, M. (1982), 'The threat of the stranger: Vulnerability, reciprocity and fieldwork', in J. Sieber (ed.), *The ethics of social research: Fieldwork, regulation and publication*, 49–70. New York: Springer Verlag.

Hynes, T. (2003), 'The issue of "trust" or "mistrust" in research with refugees: choices, caveats and considerations for researchers', *UNHCR working paper* no. 98.

Interagency Secretariat on Research Ethics (2002, 2005), The Tri-Council Policy Statement: Ethical Conduct for Research Involving Humans, Public Works and Government Services Canada (Available online at: http://pre.ethics.gc.ca /english/pdf/TCPS%20October%202005_E.pdf).

Knapik, M. (2002), 'Ethics in Qualitative Research: Searching for Practice Guidelines', paper presented at Symposium 'Linking Research to Educational Practice II', University of Calgary, Calgary, July 5–17, 2002.

Kyle, D. & Z. Liang (2001), *Migration Merchants: Organized migrant trafficking from China to Ecuador*. San Diego: Centre for Comparative Immigration Studies. University of California.

Mahler, S. (1995), *American dreaming: immigrant life on the margins*. Princeton: Princeton University Press.

Malkki, L. (1995), *Purity and exile. Violence, memory and national cosmology among Hutu refugees in Tanzania*. Chicago: University of Chicago Press.

RSC (Refugee Studies Centre) (2007), 'Ethical Guidelines for Good Research Practice', *Refugee Survey Quarterly*, Vol. 26 (3): 162–172.

Salt, J. & J. Stein (1997), 'Migration as a business: The case of trafficking', *International Migration*, 35 (4): 467–489.

Schloenhardt, A. (2001), *Trafficking in migrants: illegal migration and organised crime in Australia and the Asia Pacific region*. Leiden: Nijhoff Publishers.

Smith, L.T. (2002), Decolonizing Methodologies: Research and Indigenous Peoples, London: Zed Books.

Smythe, W.E. & M.J. Murray (2000), 'Owning the Story: Ethical considerations in narrative research', *Ethics & Behavior*, 10 (4): 311–337.

Staring, R. (2001), *Reizen onder regie. Het migratieproces van illegale Turken in Nederland*. Amsterdam: Het Spinhuis.

Witzel, A. (2000), 'The problem-centred interview', *Forum Qualitative Sozialforschung / Forum: Qualitative Social Research* 1(1). Available at: http://www.qualitative-research.net/fqs-texte/1-00/1-00witzel-e.htm.

Zetter, R. (1991), 'Labelling refugees: forming and transforming a bureaucratic identity', *Journal of Refugee Studies*, 4 (12): 39–62.

PART THREE

The Role of the Researcher

6

The 'Insider' Position: Ethical Dilemmas and Methodological Concerns in Researching Undocumented Migrants with the Same Ethnic Background

EUGENIA MARKOVA

T his chapter identifies some of the main ethical dilemmas and methodological problems that I was confronted with while studying the way undocumented Bulgarian migrants fared on the labour markets of three countries and four cities. My research focussed on Greece, Athens, Spain, Madrid, and on Brighton and London in the United Kingdom. These were primarily quantitative studies, which in the course of the research grew up to encompass a variety of qualitative methods, including participant observations, field diaries and numerous lengthy conversations and in-depth interviews with respondents. In all the studies I shared the common ethnic origin of being Bulgarian with my respondents.

The first research was a PhD research in economics financed by the European Commission ACE-PHARE programme exploring the factors determining undocumented Bulgarian immigrants' participation in the labour market of Greece. The second and the third were both post-doctoral research projects funded by the European Commission, and their aims were to examine the effects of changes in immigration status on the Bulgarian immigrants' working and living conditions in Spain and the UK respectively. The main methodological challenge from the outset of all the projects at hand was the lack of a random sampling frame. Bloch (2004) and Tait (2006) have commented on how the lack of a sampling frame for recent immigrants and refugees makes it difficult to design a statistically significant sample. The size and distribution of the undocumented migrant population in most host countries is almost never known. In Europe, Spain can be pointed out as an exception where undocumented migrants are encouraged to register at the municipalities. Still, not everybody would register there. At best there are rough estimates based on police expulsions or court cases. In the three research projects at hand, respondents were identified and interviewed using a snowball method. This method is often used when a sensitive topic is studied and when the study group is hidden, elusive, deviant or rare (Lee 1993). Undocumented labour migrants constitute such a group, one that can not be researched relying on probability samples. Similar to researching lesbian women and gay men (Platzer & James 1997), even if it was possible to screen the entire population and produce a random sample, undocumented migrants by and large would not reveal themselves under such circumstances. When the total population is not known, snowballing is the method to be used. It should be noted that the research in Spain and the UK only involved gatekeepers, who were used for providing access only and were not interviewed for the research.

In the conduct of the three research projects we had to acknowledge that 'the impossibility of obtaining a random sample is irrelevant' (Harris 2004: 17). Jacobsen & Landau (2003) discuss at least two problems with this approach, one methodological and one ethical. Unless done very carefully, the snowball procedure has the potential to include people within specific networks and to exclude others, producing biased research findings and subsequent analysis (Zulauf 1999; Arber 1993). To avoid the selection bias, to some degree, the use of recruitment from diverse sources as well as personal referrals is recommended, acknowledging the fact that the obtained sample may not be random but might include diverse segments of the undocumented migrant population (Bloch 2004; Martin & Dean 1993 in Platzer & James 1997). Ethically, the snowballing procedure increases the risk of revealing sensitive and potentially damaging information to members of a certain network; for instance, levels of poverty or access to opportunities can also be revealed in ways that may negatively affect respondents' relationships with each other (Jacobsen & Landau 2003). As I was the one conducting all interviews, I from the very beginning stuck to the principle of never discussing respondent's issues with others, including even members of their close families. I would always require that the interviews were done privately, when there were no other known people present. Exceptions were done only for couples, upon their request.

The remainder of the chapter discusses some methodological concerns about representativeness, bias and the lack of statistical data available on undocumented migrant populations. I also explore some ethical dilemmas surrounding the issues of 'social lying', befriending interviewees, potential gender 'hazards' and dealing with journalists while relating to people in vulnerable circumstances (undocumented migrant workers) and when the common characteristic between these people and the interviewer was the country of origin.

The Data Collection in Athens, Madrid,
London and Brighton

In all projects under consideration, I was collecting the data from the position of the 'insider' in the Bulgarian migrant community, sharing with my
respondents a common Bulgarian origin and, pertinent to it, language.
Many argue in favour of the 'insiderness' for the benefit of the research
process. Herself being a Croatian in Australia, Colic-Preisker (2004)
found it appropriate and even comfortable to study and represent
Croatians because she was in the unique position to earn her insider's
status primarily on the basis of language and cultural practices she was
familiar with 'by accident of [her] birth and early life in the coastal part of
Croatia' (Colic-Preisker: 143). She felt that if she was to give them a voice,
'it might be a more authentic one than what a non-Croatian ethnographer
could produce' (ibid. 143). Common language is a major determinant of
'insiderness'. It is often the crucial factor in the community's willingness
to accept an ethnic researcher. Moreover, interviewing in the respondents'
own language puts them in an easier situation (Bousetta in an interview
with De Tona on the 'race of interviewer effect' in De Tona 2006). In other
cases, a researcher can earn their 'insider's' status not only through a shared
ethnic origin and language but simply through being a foreigner in a place,
a migrant like the subjects of one's research. 'I am not saying that only
migrants can research migrants but the thing is that this knowledge gives
us the added insight', says Ronit Letona in an interview with De Tona (De
Tona 2006).

Nevertheless, the interviewers' 'inside' position can never be independent of other social categories such as age, class, regional affiliation,
educational background etc. The role of those factors and my strategies of
managing them are further discussed in the remaining chapter, in the
context of my research experience. The data collection process in Greece
started in the spring/summer of 1996, in Athens, which, at that time, was
the hub of undocumented immigrants from neighbouring countries,
including Bulgarians. There were only estimates about their numbers.
According to figures of the Athens Labour Centre (EKA), published in
1993, there were about 7,000 undocumented Bulgarians in Greece in
1993, out of a total of 66,000 illegal immigrants (excluding the large
numbers of Albanians). At that time there were almost no Bulgarians
legally employed in the country (excluding those from mixed marriages
with natives or other EU citizens), and no regularization of illegal
foreigners was even anticipated.[1] The survey had an extended and costly
preliminary part when I started establishing personal contacts with some
undocumented Bulgarian immigrants, assisting them throughout their job-
searching process or in employment-related problematic situations.

The first sample consisted of 100 undocumented Bulgarian immigrants in the Athens area of Greece, interviewed in May-September 1996 on the basis of a questionnaire containing 88 coded questions covering variables relating to four main questions. It laid the grounds for a second survey, conducted in the period March-May 1999, mainly in the Athens area while a small part of it was done in the village of Moires, on the island of Crete. The second survey was designed in view of the regularization of the stay and work of 'illegal' foreigners in Greece initiated by the Greek government in January 1998. 153 Bulgarian immigrants were questioned. The survey used a questionnaire containing 128 coded questions covering variables related to five main questions.

The purposive or snowballing method of sampling was employed also in the second survey. In order to minimise the risk of a biased sample, particular care was taken for as many entry points as possible to be used for accessing the interviewees. Furthermore, in order to produce a data set that permits comparative analysis, a control group was included in the sample – Bulgarian immigrants who had managed to regularise their immigration status. The acquaintances from the fieldwork in 1996 proved to be very helpful and the survey's preliminary part for building trust between the interviewer and the immigrants was considerably shortened. Moreover, the first study in 1996 put the beginning of my very personal involvement with the Bulgarian migrant community in Greece, which further deepened with the study in 1999, namely, through the establishment of the first Bulgarian migrant organisation in Greece, 'Vassil Levski', and a Sunday school for Bulgarian migrant children. Some people argue that the active involvement of the researcher with the community under study can influence the interviewees' responses and produce compromising findings (Jacobsen and Landau 2003). I argue that such active involvement with the Bulgarian migrant community actually provided me with access to people who would not have been accessed otherwise because they were not members of any social groups and they were not visiting places where Bulgarian tended to congregate; some of them were practically 'enslaved' by their employers and were not allowed to go out. I only met them because they rang me calling for help. Although the two samples in Greece were by no means representative, they offered an instructive picture of the undocumented Bulgarians' characteristics and labour market behaviour.

The data collection processes in Spain (2003–2004) and in the UK (2004) were a very different experience as I was an 'outsider' for the Bulgarian economic migrant community there. Sharing the same country of origin and language were not enough to make me an 'insider' to the Bulgarian community in Madrid. For this reason, the survey in Spain, as the first one in Greece in 1996, involved an extensive and expensive preliminary part with the objective to locate Bulgarian migrant' locations in Madrid and gain access to them through the establishment of personal contacts with the so-called gatekeepers (influential people among the Bulgarian community there). They provided access to Bulgarian-owned businesses ('phone and money houses', (*locutorios* in Spanish), coffee shops, restaurants), where immigrants usually gathered. Some other interviews were conducted in private in the migrants' houses. To minimise the bias in the sample, gatekeepers were not surveyed. My age, gender, class and educational background assumed increased importance in the way I was establishing contacts with potential respondents or gatekeepers, who were carefully scrutinising me. Once, a Bulgarian woman who was regularly organising Sunday lunches at her flat for many of her Bulgarian friends got interested in my research. She invited me to one of her Sunday gatherings with the intention to introduce me to her friends. Quite inconsiderately and against the Bulgarian tradition, I turned up there holding no gift and worst of all, wearing a newly bought leather jacket. To my huge embarrassment, the visit turned into a 'trial' where the woman was questioning me in front of her friends about my job and earnings. I survived the awkwardness of the situation and even managed to get a second invite. I realised that the host had invited me more as a visitor than a researcher. The rules of social visiting required that I had a small gift for the hosts; I needed to disclose bits and pieces of my own migration story to 'break the ice' (Colic-Preisker 2004). However, this also taught me a change in my strategy – to be more cautious with the Bulgarian women about class differences and when in the field to always dress similar to the way these women, who were doing hard manual work in Spanish homes, were dressing. Similar strategy was followed by Madriz (1997) when researching Latin women and crime; she needed to reduce the visible class differences by changing her dressing style and adapting it to the one of her respondents.

The Spanish sample consisted of 202 Bulgarian immigrants, over the age of 18, living in the Madrid area (particularly, in the southern suburbs of Getafe and Parla, and in the south-eastern region of Alkala de Henares). They were interviewed in November-December 2003, and in April 2004, shortly after the train blasts at Attocha station in Madrid, with a questionnaire, containing some 130 coded variables relating to 5 main questions. Even though Spanish Municipalities had data on the numbers of Bulgarian undocumented migrants registered there that theoretically would have allowed us the design of a proper random sample, the insecurity of migrants' legal status made the application of the random procedure irrelevant. Purposive sampling was applied instead. The survey in the UK (London and Brighton) also relied on gatekeepers for securing access to Bulgarian immigrants; unlike in Spain or Greece, there were no particular concentrations of Bulgarian immigrants and most interviews were conducted in private homes allowing the access to otherwise 'difficult-to-access' or 'hard-to-reach' people (see Introduction to this book); 111 immigrants were surveyed and all interviews were conducted in Bulgarian.

The survey instruments were available in Bulgarian and Bulgarian was the original language of the questionnaires as well. The fact that I as a native Bulgarian speaker was conducting the interviews potentially reduced the risk of biased responses that often occur as a result of using translators (see also Dahinden & Efionayi-Mäder in this book) .

Nonetheless, it should be recognised that the 'insider' position bears the risk of trapping the researcher into always studying the same communities. Escaping this 'trap' enables researchers to utilise their experience to approach other communities and study those different to their own populations, which can produce valuable comparative research. At the same time, being an 'insider' researcher can be a very lonely experience lacking the team work where research strategies, achievements and failures are collectively shared. Moreover, it is always safer to interview in pairs or even bigger groups in higher-risk situations.

Issues of Ethical Concern

Manipulation: how far can we go?

I believe it is not realistic to assume that fieldwork can always proceed very smoothly on some ideal level of perfect truth. As Joan Cassell (1982) writes, and I would agree with her, 'fieldwork, like friendship requires a number of social lies to keep interaction flowing fairly smoothly'. Because fieldwork involves face-to-face interactions with real people and as it is difficult to predict people's moods, intentions and reactions, it is equally difficult to predict how an interview can develop.

Sometimes, a few social lies are necessary elements of the process of accessing and studying undocumented immigrants. For example, I started my research on undocumented immigrants in Athens in 1996 through two women from my home city in Bulgaria, who used to be regular customers of my parents' pharmacy. My mum gave them my phone number in Athens and they immediately contacted me after facing problems with recruitment agencies, all of which were functioning outside the law, or with employers who were not paying them and were unlawfully keeping their passports. These were the first two women I interviewed for my research and they served as 'guarantors' for accessing other respondents. Because of my frequent involvement in solving their problems with employers and agencies, we became friends. On a few occasions they'd asked me to accompany them to the recruitment agency to help them with Greek into Bulgarian translation. I saw it as a unique opportunity to examine from 'inside' how these illegal recruitment structures functioned. It was not possible to constantly remind these women that apart from helping them I was actually doing my research. And, to the administrators and managers of these illegal recruitment agencies I was introduced as another Bulgarian woman who was accompanying her friends but who was not looking for a job. Clearly, this experience can be classified as 'covert' research. Social research is not normally covert but since it involved the study of hidden and illegal issues (illegal recruitment of illegal worker and illegal 'selling' of their labour to employers in the illegal economy), it could not be studied using other conventional open methods. I had the unique chance, for a couple of hours, to observe how these agencies were functioning; I saw some of their clients and even talked to a few of the immigrants without documents who were waiting there for a job from the agency.

The question of boundaries between the interviewer and the respondents

Through my migrant friends I accessed places, people and information I could not have gotten otherwise. By strict ethical standards, using friendship for obtaining information should be considered a form of deception. The reason for this, some argue, is that researchers who 'become deeply involved and familiar with their informants' (Kloos 1969) – through the methodological problem known as reactivity – will contribute towards a distorted research process, producing biased information and compromised findings (Jacobsen & Landau 2003). Apparently, these concerns stem from the assumption that 'it's un-ethical to give in a context defined by power differences, because giving further exacerbates these differences and, for one thing, may lure people into participating in a project that they may otherwise have preferred to stay away from' (Lammers 2007: 75).

Researchers, whether filling in questionnaires or conducting more in-depth interviews, always hope to establish trustworthy relationships with their respondents in order to obtain reliable, truthful answers to produce as credible a research as possible. Establishing trust with respondents usually takes time and involves respect. 'It is context-dependent how trust and respect are obtained and expressed, but it usually has something to do with dynamics of giving and receiving' (Lammers 2005: 8). This can involve giving of your time to listen to them, sharing intimacies about one's own life, translating for them or providing them with information about changes in the immigration law, or information on their human and employment rights as undocumented migrants, assisting them in hospital, or simply sharing a cup of coffee or a meal with them. Nonetheless, it's been recognised that better data about people's experiences and feelings are generated through an open and reciprocal relationship between the researcher and the people being interviewed. This inevitably involves disclosure on the part of the researcher (Platzer & James 1997).

Once getting to know more and more Bulgarians in Athens, all without documents and always frightened, and on the alert for police checks, I found it really hard, even uncomfortable to distance myself from these people, when, in fact, I was in a privileged position (residence permit, office and financial support to do a PhD at the University of Athens, and a comfortable home I shared with my then Greek partner) to be able to alleviate some of their troubles. Feminist researchers emphasize 'the importance of establishing non-hierarchical relationships with intervie-wees' (Oakey 1981: 44) given that there are common characteristics between the researcher and the researched (McKay & Snyder 2008). I and the people I was surveying shared a major commonality – the country of origin, which entailed common language and similar experiences, at least with people of similar age. However, the 'non-hierarchical relationship' was not applicable because it could not be sustained through the survey process which involved trust-building and trust-maintaining throughout, and involved the 'dynamics of giving and receiving' (Lammers 2005: 8).

It was impressive to learn that I was not alone in my decision to get involved with the undocumented Bulgarian migrants in Athens, providing them with practical assistance. At a later time and in a different context, another researcher, Ellen Lammers – studying young refugee men in Uganda – had decided in favour of 'giving' as opposed to 'no giving' to her research respondents. Faced with the destitute situation of many of her respondents, Lammers (2007) found herself paying for a variety of things for her respondents, from passport size photos to letters of recommenda-tion, appeal, request and complaint to be typed and posted, to blood tests, hospital bills, monthly rents, and even school fees; she was also engaged in hands-on advocacy work. Similarly, I faced other facets of human suffering – people whose passports were kept unlawfully by exploitative employers and who could not cross the border to go home and see their children for years, or attend funerals of loved ones; people, working as carers and baby sitters, who were kept 24 hours at employers' disposal and not allowed to go out; people, seriously ill who could not go the doctor of fears to not be reported to the police. Lammers' respondents were young refugees, who refused to live in refugee settlements in remote rural areas, and resided in Kampala illegally, not entitled to any form of humanitarian assistance, and without even ID to prove who they were. My respondents were Bulgarian men and women of all ages, from 18 to over 60, who, at that time, had left their country for economic reasons, to provide for starving family and chil-dren; they had no legal documents to reside and work in Greece because there were no legal channels available for that, thus living in constant fear of apprehension and extradition, and often subjected to exploitation by unscrupulous employers. Lammers' respondents and mine shared a distinct similarity – both groups lacked security.

My gradual involvement with the Bulgarian immigrant community in Athens started from meetings that combined filling in questionnaires with having a cup of tea and/or being an attentive listener. Naturally, later on,

I started disclosing some personal information especially with respondents my age. After a few months, I began to take part in consultancy sessions for undocumented migrants organised by the trade unions in Athens (e.g. informing migrants on their employment and human rights) and in advocacy activities organised by unions and anti-racist organisations (e.g. taking migrant cases to trade union and immigration lawyers; advocating and negotiating for migrant legalisation). At that time, some accused me of crossing boundaries with my respondents because of my emotional and practical involvement to help them, which was well beyond my research tasks. However, at that time I believed and I still believe that there was not any other way to do it. As my research was not posing any harm to the people under study and it was not violating their autonomy, I argue it is acceptable. Quantitative results were only publicised based on large samples, with no indicative information provided as to particular characteristics of respondents or locations they usually gathered. Moreover, my research provided much needed knowledge about the conditions of life and work of undocumented workers, the agencies' mechanisms of functioning that were recruiting them and then 'selling' them to dubious employers in the 'shadow' economy. Others criticised my research work as the product of befriending respondents thus making it distorted, partial and far from neutral. It's comforting to know that an increasing number of sociologists and anthropologists acknowledge a more human and flexible approach to research that 'requires us to be conscious of the ways we are involved and engaged with our research participants', looking for ethical strategies to manage that engagement (Colic-Preisker 2004: 83), when neutrality is 'neither obligatory nor desirable' (Lammers 2005:7).

To sum up, I believe that conducting fieldwork, even as an economist and not as an anthropologist can be a very personal experience and emotional involvement seems inevitable. Such an involvement provides the grounds for an in-depth knowledge of the life and work of people in precarious conditions; it also expands considerably the pull of people that can be surveyed; it allows for panel surveys through the securing of a continuous contact with the interviewees; it also creates personal relationships that I cherish to date. These personal contacts can not be traded. That is why I found it unacceptable when a few months ago a colleague from another University asked me to pass them some of my East European contacts, preferably undocumented immigrants, in Brighton.

The meaning of gender in safety and access strategies

Another issue on access of undocumented migrants touches upon the very narrow difference between what is ethical and un-ethical between a female interviewer and a male respondent, given that both parties are heterosexual. Conaway (1986) wonders as to why her courses or seminars had

EUGENIA MARKOVA

not ever acknowledged the fact that the researcher's gender norms and sexuality definitely impact data collection when there is no such thing as a 'neutral researcher', especially when 'you are much too young to be genderless'. Conaway's strategy was to appear less feminine by local standards and therefore less 'available'. Giovanni (1986), another young woman, doing her anthropological research in a small Sicilian town, had to live with a family to gain the confidence of local people; however, in order to minimize bias by having only women informants, she needed other tactics to access men as well; as a result, her only male informant put his 'social worth' in jeopardy to assist her. My male informants in Madrid were less willing to do so and my safety strategy was to get my questionnaire completed by as many respondents as possible but in public places and never in men's homes. On one occasion, late in the evening when interviewing in a Bulgarian phone shop ('*locutorio*') in the southern poor suburbs of Madrid, I managed to persuade a man, about my age, to sit and fill in a questionnaire. He did it and then, somewhat in exchange of my 'invite to fill in a questionnaire', asked me to go with him to a night club. Naturally, I declined. He got upset even angry and then aggressive – he could not understand why I would not go out with him when he actually did the questionnaire for me even though he felt too tired and unwilling initially. It's inevitable that some [relatively young] male respondents will form certain expectations from a [relatively young] woman researcher when they decide to participate in her study. I found a 'safe exit' out of an apparently delicate situation. It was not so much about my personal safety but rather the 'personal worth' of the man. His self-esteem had to be protected. What proved helpful was that we both spoke Bulgarian and there were no friends of his around; only the shop owner was present; it is always easier to be more persuasive in one's mother tongue. On another occasion, I managed to gain access to one of the influential men in the Bulgarian undocumented migrant community there. He felt so comfortable with me that even volunteered information about his involvement in a gang copying credit cards in restaurants; he wanted to protect me by saying that I should always pay in cash in Madrid and never use my credit card. I could not agree with his activities but I considered it unreasonable to contradict him, which to me was another necessary 'deceit'. In fact, I was faced with another difficulty linked to my implicitly condoning his illegal activities; the idea of doing no harm to my respondents prevailed. Then he suggested, even demanded to introduce me to his peers who were also without documents and I would imagine they were also involved in similar activities. But, I had to go to his house for this, he said, where he was planning to gather them all. Again, lies and a certain degree of acceptable manipulation were needed for me to avoid doing that but without loosing his trust because first, he was an important 'gatekeeper' in the community and, second, for my own safety. In principle, for a female researcher to be in a house alone with a man she barely knows poses an increased risk of harm. As an extreme example, Eva Moreno (1995) unconsciously created the conditions to be alone in a house with a similar age male research assistant; eventually he raped her. Moreno followed a strategy that would not impose strict boundaries and treat all people working with her as equal, ignoring to a degree cultural specificities. These are cases that exemplify two situations – one that has the potential to harm the interviewer and another one that has already caused the harm. In order for such situations to be prevented, the use of lies about non-existing commitments and an invented family status (e.g. being married is always safer), I considered necessary during such phases of the fieldwork. Such examples reveal the vulnerability of both respondents and researchers, and the importance of creating a relationship that would enhance trust, which requires time and this is not always feasible. They also show that researchers of undocumented migrants are continuously faced with ethical dilemmas throughout the whole research process, and beyond it, especially when issues of access and 'gatekeeping' are involved.

Responsibilities over dissemination of data and research findings

It is in the *use* of research findings that the potential harm for the participants in the survey lies. The main risks of harm are invasion of privacy and breach of confidentiality. Working with undocumented immigrants is a serious affair, because they can be arrested by the immigration authorities, imprisoned and even extradited from the country. Such harm is however less immediate and difficult to predict while conducting the actual research. A main concern with confidentiality in sensitive research[2] is that the unique and personal nature of the data may make it easy for participants to be identified in research reports by themselves and others (Brannen 1988 cited in Platzer & James 1997). In my research projects, I found that respondents had this concern – more in smaller locations (the city of Brighton in the UK and the village of Moires, Crete in Greece) than in capital cities (Athens, Madrid and London) – mainly about being identified by immigration and police officers with authority to arrest, imprison and expel. The primarily quantitative nature of the study – large samples of minimum 100 respondents – was in itself a protection; results were summarised in tables and presented in numbers; they were supplemented by personal stories which were not revealing such unique data that may point to a particular individual. To me, many of the most serious risks are actually posed not necessarily at the dissemination stage but much earlier, sometime during or after the data collection phase when inconsiderate, blatant journalists approach the research team to ask for 'raw data' –

contacts of respondents to be used in journalistic investigations. A fresh example: one month ago I was contacted by the researcher of a popular night show on British TV. The reason I was contacted was my involvement in the Joseph Rowntree Foundation funded research project on East European immigration and community cohesion in the UK. At that time the first draft of the final report was just produced. So, the researcher of this show started asking me whether we had interviewed any undocumented immigrants amongst the studied groups. This very question alarmed me that their intentions could not be good; besides, I've learned that journalists will always write in strict compliance with the beliefs of their newspaper. I answered with 'Yes, we did find undocumented migrants and they were amongst those and those groups'; besides, this information was also available in the draft report. Then, the TV researcher continued 'Do they work in cleaning?' 'Some of them do', I answered. And then the very blunt question: 'Can you give me their phone numbers? I want to talk to them?' – a few long seconds of silence on my end. I was startled. To keep it polite and save time I mentioned: 'These people have difficulties speaking English'. The TV person immediately replied: 'No problem; we have interpreters/colleagues here that speak all these languages'. Of course, I did not give them any phone numbers. They understood I won't be of much help and did not waste time with me. I found this experience quite disturbing, in fact. How they could have even thought that I or anybody studying undocumented migrants would give the phone numbers of their respondents? It's against the very basic ethical principles of privacy and confidentiality in research. Obviously, they found other 'informants' as later on that day, the news programme in question revealed that there were undocumented cleaners working in the buildings of the Home Office: their big news was that undocumented workers were actually working for the government, alarming the public and urging the politicians to do something about it (implying these people should be extradited). The moral of the story is very obvious. I gave this example not as my personal ethical dilemma but as one possible ethical dilemma that would certainly be encountered by people involved in research, examining such sensitive issues as legal immigration status. On another occasion, when the final report of the same JRF study on East European immigrants and community cohesion in the UK was finally published, many newspapers ignored our positive messages and instead, gave their own interpretation of certain results, in fact manipulating the research findings, in order to present to the public an image of 'not willing to integrate'. Other journalists are truly professional in reporting migrant research findings. Researchers can do little to affect journalists' professionalism. However, they can do a lot to protect the communities they study by assuring anonymity and total confidentiality of their respondents.

Conclusion

Being a researcher who comes from the same country of origin as the undocumented migrants under study can be hugely beneficial in minimizing the sample bias as it eliminates the need for translations. However, this can pose a danger for steering towards the 'advocacy research' direction where the researchers sharing such a commonality with the researched as the country of origin go to the research fields to 'prove' their pre-defined hypothesis. Researchers need to be open and willing to be proven wrong (Jacobsen & Landau 2003). It's worth repeating that there is no unique methodology for ethically collecting robust and credible data. Several ethical and methodological concerns have been outlined in the chapter exemplifying the need for following the methods and standards of not only one discipline (see also Introduction to this book). Yet, what's valid for all research – a research method is ethically stronger when it can protect the anonymity of the surveyed respondents and it is methodologically weaker when it fails to inform policy based on biased results of a limited non-random sample.

Notes

1 At that time and up until 1998, immigration in Greece was regulated by L. 1975/1991 considered to be one of the most restrictive in Europe.
2 In this chapter, researching undocumented migration is considered as sensitive a research as researching gay men and lesbian women.

Bibliography

Arber, S. (1993), 'The research process', in N. Gilbert (ed.), *Researching Social Life*, 32–50. London: Sage Publications.

Bloch, A. (2004), 'Survey Research with Refugees, a methodological perspective', *Policy Studies*, Vol. 25 (2): 139–151.

Cassell, J, (1982), 'Harms, Benefits, Wrongs, and Rights in Fieldwork', in J. Sieber (ed.), *The Ethics of Social Research: Fieldwork, Regulation and Publication*, 7–31. New York: Springler-Verlag.

Colic-Preisker, V. (2004), 'Doing Ethnography in "One's Own Ethnic Community": The Experience of an Awkward Insider', in L. Hume and J. Mulcock (eds.), *Anthropologists in the Field: Cases in Participant Observation*, 82–95. New York: Columbia University Press.

Conaway, M.E. (1986), 'The Pretence of a Neutral Researcher', in T.L. Whitehead & M.E. Conaway (eds.), *Self, Sex and Gender in Cross-Cultural Fieldwork*, 52–64. Urbana and Chicago: University of Illinois Press.

Giovanni, M. (1986), 'Female Anthropologist and Male Informant', in T.L. Whitehead & M.E. Conaway (eds.), *Self, Sex and Gender in Cross-Cultural Fieldwork*, 103–116. Urbana and Chicago: University of Illinois Press.

Harris, H. (2004), 'The Somali Community in the UK: What we know and how we know it', London: Information Centre About Asylum and Refugees (ICAR).

Jacobsen, K. & L.B. Landau (2003), 'The Dual Imperative in Refugee Research: Some Methodological and Ethical Considerations in Social Science Research on Forced Migration'. *Disasters*, Vol. 27 (3): 185–206.

Kloos, P. (1969), 'Role Conflicts in Social Fieldwork', *Current Anthropology*, Vol. 10 (5): 509–512.

Lammers, E. (2005), 'Refugees, asylum seekers and anthropologists: the taboo on giving'. *Global Migration Perspectives*, no. 29, April 2005, Global Commission on International Migration.

Lammers, E. (2007), 'Researching Refugees: Preoccupations with Power and Questions of Giving', *Refugee Survey Quarterly*, Vol. 26 (3): 72–81.

Lee, R.M. (1993), *Doing Research on Sensitive Issues*. London: Sage Publications.

Madriz, E. (1997), *Nothing Bad Happens to Good Girls: Fear of Crime in Women's Lives*, Berkely: University of California Press.

Moreno, E. (1995), 'Rape in the field: reflections from a survivor', in D. Kulick & M. Wilson (eds.) *Taboo: Sex, Identity and Erotic Subjectivity in Anthropological Fieldwork*, 219–250. London and New York: Routledge.

McKay, S. & P. Snyder (2008), 'Methodological challenges in researching the working experiences of refugees and recent migrants', in S. McKay (ed.), *Refugees, Recent Migrants and Employment: Challenging Barriers and Exploring Pathways*, New York: Routledge.

Oakey, A. (1981), 'Interviewing women: a contradiction in terms', in H. Roberts (ed.), *Doing Feminist Research*, 83–113. London: Routledge and Kegan Paul.

Platzer, H. & T. James (1997), 'Methodological issues conducting sensitive research on lesbian and gay men's experience of nursing care', *Journal of Advanced Nursing*, Vol. 25: 626–633.

Tait, K. (2006), 'Refugee voices as evidence in policy and practice', in Temple, B. & R. Moran (eds.) *Doing research with refugees: issues and guidelines*, 133–154. Bristol: Policy Press.

Zulauf, M. (1999), 'Cross-national qualitative research: accommodation ideals and reality', *International Journal of Social Research Methodology*, Vol. 2 (2): 159–169.

7

The Fieldworker as Social Worker: Dilemma's in Research with Moroccan Unaccompanied Minors in Spain

Núria Empez

In Spain, at the end of the 1990s, mostly in big cities such as Barcelona and Madrid, Moroccan minors started to appear, hanging about in the streets. These minors, mostly boys between fifteen to eighteen years old, had migrated alone, without the company of any responsible adult. This chapter is based on research I conducted on the migration processes of these unaccompanied minors. My research is part of my PhD dissertation. I began the research in 2001 and it is still ongoing at the moment of writing this chapter (in 2008).

The group I am researching consists of minors, which in itself requires a very careful processing (see for example Hopkins 2008). In addition the unaccompanied minors in question were staying in Spain in 'irregular administrative situations'. They had entered the country in illegal ways, but as minors they have found themselves under the protection of the state. This protection however is not indefinite; they could stay in Spain, at least until they are 18 and if they are not deported for example for family reunification reasons. This precarious situation of the people I want to research is in many ways methodologically but also ethically challenging. Another challenge I faced was the aim of looking at the phenomenon from a transnational perspective, which meant doing fieldwork in both sending as well as receiving countries, in my case Morocco and Spain. I was of the opinion that this was the only way to truly understand the migration processes of these minors. But little has been written so far on transnational research methods. In the contact I had with these minors I was also playing a double role. Something else I was struggling with was that I am an anthropologist on the one hand and a social worker on the other. This double role provides several advantages, but at the same time involves dilemmas which have to be faced and solved throughout the research process. The aim of this chapter is to analyze the difficulties when we are investigating children in 'administrative irregular situations' when doing multi-sited research and when researchers have a double role in the sense that they are also engaged as social workers as I was.

Motivations for starting this research

Research is never neutral; when we start an investigation we always have a preconceived idea of the field we want to explore. My research started in 2001 when I returned from a year and a half of fieldwork with street children in Managua, Nicaragua, Central America, to Barcelona (Spain), my homeland. My initial idea was to write my PhD thesis on street children in Nicaragua. But to my surprise the Spanish newspapers were talking about a new phenomenon: the recent appearance of street children in Madrid and Barcelona. I reacted with disbelief, how was it possible that children are living in the streets in a developed country such as Spain? What motivated me to initiate this research was that the Spanish Government was ignoring these children, especially the ones without papers. This last group of minors saw themselves confronted with two different laws in Spain, one of protection: 'Child protection rights', and another one of control: 'Foreigners Law'. The last law was often the most felt by those living on the street and seemed to overrule the first one.

Difficulties with definitions

In this chapter I'm going to focus on methodological and ethical difficulties of research on the topic of unaccompanied minors. But before that I want to pay some attention to the conceptual dilemmas in my field of research. We need to know what we are talking about before we can start the actual research. So what is an unaccompanied minor? I could use the definition of the European Union (EU) that describes them as:

> Third-country nationals below the age of eighteen, who arrive on the territory of the Member States unaccompanied by an adult responsible for them whether by law or custom, and for as long as they are not effectively in the care of such a person.[1]

The Convention on the Rights of the Child (1989) describes them in article 20.1 as:

> A child temporarily or permanently deprived of his or her family environment, or in whose own best interests cannot be allowed to remain in that environment, shall be entitled to special protection and assistance provided by the State.

Following the EU definition or the Convention on the Rights of Children definition one would expect these minors to be treated the same everywhere. But when we dig into it we see that unaccompanied minors face different laws and treaties in different countries. If we look at how different European countries treat their unaccompanied minors many differences come to light. Germany and Great Britain for example treat unaccompanied minors as asylum seekers. They call them: 'unaccompanied asylum seekers', or 'unaccompanied refugee minors'. Spain and Italy apply general child-related protection laws to them. They are called '*menores no acompañados*' resp. '*miniori strangieri non acompagnati*', both referring to minors who are unaccompanied (Quiroga 2003, Jiminez 2004, 2006, Empez 2003, 2007). Belgium combines both perspectives of asylum and protection of minors. And France does not have any special treatment for these children; they are integrated in the resources from the common law of children protection. They are called '*mineurs isoles*' without reference to their migration past (Conred 2005, Senovilla 2007).

Difficulties with statistical data

In my research, I focus on minors who came alone, without any responsible adult, most of them hiding under a truck or a bus crossing the shores of the 'Estrecho de Gibraltar' in a ferry boat, from their departure country (Morocco) to Spain. I concentrated on the Community of Catalonia,[2] because it is together with Madrid and Andalucia the community where most immigrants reside and as such is where most unaccompanied minors are likely to go. The phenomena of children migrating alone started to be visible in Spain around 1998, with a big impact in the press in the years 2000 and 2001, generating enormous attention from different instances and disciplines such as journalists, social workers, jurists and anthropologists. Many estimates were made. A study carried out by ConRed, a virtual community aimed at preventing violence against immigrant children and adolescents who have no social support network[3] show for example that there are 30,000 unaccompanied minors throughout 17 countries of Europe. They estimated 1000 to 2000 new children per year in Spain, with an average age of 14–15 years. However for several reasons it is not easy to quantify the phenomenon of migration of unaccompanied minors. First of all these children are very mobile and move from one place to the other making it hard to 'capture' them in a database. Secondly, not all of them end up in the protection system. And thirdly those who do end up in the protection system may have lied about their true identity and can easily have been counted more than once. Fourthly the way data is collected differs from time and time and from country to country and there is no coherent system. And finally, some unaccompanied minors may have found some of their family members in the country of destination and are no longer unaccompanied even when they are still in the database. Regardless of all these difficulties, some data provided by the Catalan Children Protection Authorities is listed below.

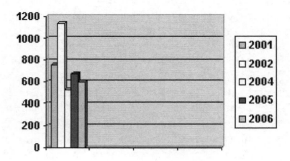

Figure 8.1   Number of unaccompanied minors in Catalonia, 2001–2006

This graph refers to the number of estimated unaccompanied minors who attend the Catalan welfare system per year. In Spain, the responsibilities, or 'competences', for child protection is placed on the autonomic level. Provinces are individually responsible for the protection of children while the foreigner's 'competences' are handled by the state government. That means that in this case Catalonia is the administration in charge to give protection to the children. Every autonomic province however has arranged the protection system in its own way. Hence we can find differences in the way that children are treated as well as counted from one province to another. In general this data must be used as orientation, because is difficult to know the exact number of unaccompanied children. The government reports different official numbers referring to the same year and we can even find different data coming from the same source.

Besides, these numbers only refer to the minors who got in contact with the protection system, omitting the unaccompanied minors that never showed up in the protection system. The advantage of using a qualitative research approach is that I am able to contact all kinds of unaccompanied minors, the ones within the protection system, the ones who are out of it and the ones that alternate in and out of it. While using this approach I got to know mostly boys, but also some girls that came as unaccompanied minors, and live with some family members (not parents or legal tutors but brothers, sisters, uncles, etc.).

Research outside the protection system: an urban ethnography

Most of the publications that appear on the topic of unaccompanied minors in Spain, like Capdevila (2003, 2001), Duran (2007), Jimenez (2005, 2006), Larranga (1999), Monteros (2006) and Quiroga (2003, 2001) have failed to succeed in reaching those minors who are not known by protection centres. Even most of the anthropological research in this field that is based on fieldwork focuses on the institutions that take care of these children and does not include those who are excluded from these same institutions. The limitations of this research are clear: an important number of children is missing, children who never go there or who alternate life in the protection center with a life outside it. My intention was to make an urban ethnography, to meet the children in public space, having to avoid finding them in the minor's protection centres. In contrast to what I mentioned above, not all of the unaccompanied minors are to be found in the streets, so it is important to state that I'm not focusing on the reality of *all* members of this group. I'm showing a fragmentary, but real part of the experience of some of them. Besides, I must add, that even when I contacted the children in public spaces, most of them were within the protection system. Some had some spare time at the moment of the interview; others had escaped the protection system centres (mostly when they feared expulsion). The advantage of using this method is that I will get new insights in a side of the story that is rarely told and I will be able to complete the 'institutional reality' with this information.

For my research I followed the fieldwork principles established by the Chicago School, Thomas (1918), Park (1967, 1972, 1925) Burgess (1925). In their theories spontaneous and direct contact was the key, they invented the word participant observation. In my case this full time ethnography was impossible to do. Most of the children alternate their lives in protection centers, even some times in justice centers, with the life in the streets, making it very difficult and even impossible to share all moments in their lives as in a classical ethnography. I always tried to limit the fieldwork to public spaces, and to be accessible enough, so they could invite me to share different moments of their lives, such as taking a coffee, going to the hospital or getting to know their families. But this was just not always possible. Besides, the whole transnational aspect of my research complicated it even more.

The transnational perspective and multi-sited ethnography

We can use different approaches to the same topic; when I started the research with unaccompanied minors, in 2001 in Barcelona, I quickly understood that I was facing a transnational phenomenon, i.e. I could not understand what was going on in Barcelona without knowing what was going on back in Morocco. That is why I decided to use this approach in my research. The need for transnational studies arises to address the complexity of the globalization process, in which movements of people, goods, and capital are taking place beyond the boundaries of a nation-state. If I look at the migratory patterns in a separate way, like origin and destination, we will miss the complexity of the phenomenon and run the risk of arriving at misunderstandings or weak conclusions. One of the conclusions of my research is that changes in Spain produce changes in the patterns of migration back in Morocco and I could add the other way around as well.

I will give you one example of this interlinkage. Because of their proximity of 14 kilometres, Spain and Morocco have been related since antiquity. Before 1985, Moroccans had no need of a visa to enter Spain; the movements between the people of both countries were fluid. Some Moroccans moved to Spain to work in a temporary job such as agriculture; after the agriculture campaign they returned to Morocco; others came to study or to visit as tourists. Even if it was not possible for everyone, because it requires some wealth to move, it was relatively easy to come and go from Spain. As a condition for entering the EU in 1986, Spain created its first foreigner's Law in 1985 (*La Ley de Extranjería*) requiring, among other things, a visa for Moroccans and some other nationalities to enter the country. After the creation of this Law there were several modifications of the Law, and the regulations gradually became more restricted. With the possibilities to migrate legally to Spain closing, some people started to migrate in an irregular way.

Even for those who reach Spain, however, there are few ways to gain legal residency. One is to register in the *Padrón* (the Municipal Register) and wait for an Amnesty. This is however not covered in the law and will depend on a political decision of the Government. For each Amnesty the requirements to apply are changed. Moreover, it is uncertain when and if a new Amnesty is going to be granted. Another way to gain legal status, this one is included in the current law, is to apply for residency. This is possible if one can prove that one has been living in Spain for three continuous years and has had a job for at least one year. One also needs a relative of the first order (child, sibling or parent) with legal residence in Spain, or a social service report, and no criminal record. Because of the difficulties in fulfilling such requirements, this Law benefits very few people. For 'unaccompanied minors', children without any responsible adult, there is another option. If such children arrive in Spain, humanitarian laws governing child protection are supposed to take precedence, treating them as 'neglected' children who require the protection of the state as well as the international community,[4] and giving them the possibility of obtaining legal status. In the current *Ley de estranjería*, there is a special article referring to unaccompanied minors. The article 92, point 5, says:

> After nine months have elapsed since the minor was put in the competent services of the minors protection [system] . . . , and having once tried repatriation with his or her family or to the country of origin, and this having not been possible, [the state] will grant him or her the residence authorization to which refers the statutory law 4/2000, of 11 of January.[5]

This means that if after nine months the minor is not sent back to the country of origin, the Spanish state must provide him or her with Spanish residence, and the opportunity to stay in the country with a legal status.

Another example that migration policies in Spain affect migration patterns back in Africa could be the aftermath of the implementation of Spain's '*Sistema integral de vigilancia del Estrecho*' (SIVE) in 2002 to control the South border. Putting this in place dramatically decreased the number of boats trying to cross from Morocco to Spain, but these attempts were simply moved to more risky routes such as Mauritania and even Gambia. Irregular migration doesn't stop; attempts at prevention change the patterns coinciding with the rules and regulations that can affect it. With strict border control, and the difficulties to gain legal status in Spain, children have a window of opportunity to gain legal status if they show up in Spain as unaccompanied minors. Even if I must take into consideration that each child has his own history, motivations, and family ties, it is important to have this transnational perspective to better understand minor's movements.

I conducted fieldwork and participant observation in Spain (mostly Barcelona) and in Morocco (mostly Tangier). The longest stay in Morocco was six months in 2006,[6] but during the years there have been more than 20 short stays in different places of Morocco, especially in Tangier. I combined participant observation with informal and semi-structured interviews with minors themselves, but also with their families (in Morocco) and sometimes in Spain if they were part of a 'transnational fostering'. I started the contact with some minors and their families (back in Morocco) via snowball sampling, starting as many chains as minors I could get in contact with, and sometimes the other way around, I got to know a family in Morocco and they connected me with their child already in Catalonia as unaccompanied minor. The fieldwork is still going on, but since 2001 I have established a relationship with more than 100 unaccompanied children in Barcelona and Morocco and with more than 25 of their families. I also spoke to key informants like social workers, lawyers, NGO members, etc. in both countries. The methodology of multi-sited research that I used is not sufficiently worked out yet in the literature and

I had to face some specific obstacles that I will further elaborate on in the following paragraphs.

Working with disrupted contacts

Since 2001, when I started my research in the center of Barcelona, there were different places where the children gathered in the city. These places have been changing however due to the intervention of the police. At the beginning of my research in 2001, I found three major venues, '*Plaça Catalunya*' and '*Plaça Reial*', both of them in the city centre of Barcelona and another in Santa Coloma de Gramanet, a city close to Barcelona, where the children would gather. These places were relevant because the children used to group themselves according to origin. Even among the group of *Plaça Reial*, almost all came from the same neighbourhood in Tangier (Senia). Later on, with the intervention of the police forces, the children started to disperse, and move to more different and smaller groups. Also there are differences depending on the season of the year or the time of the day. In summer they often move to the beach areas while in winter they concentrate in the city centre. Some of them, if they are out of the protection system and live in the streets, can be sleeping in parks, abandoned cars, or what they called *Kharbas* (squatted houses) these places also change with time. The fieldwork itself taught me where you can find these children, but to maintain contact with them is however not always easy because they are in constant movement. Site selection is great when you are researching people who stay put, but in my case it was much more complicated as the sites that were important to me changed because the children were in constant movement.

It wasn't just difficult to find them within the city, but I was also confronted with mobility of the children between cities, autonomous communities and even between countries. The pressure of the children to arrange their administrative situation and the mistrust they sometimes had in the protection system can be reasons for that movement. We can find different flows of children to different cities of Spain where they think they can arrange their administrative situation, or where they think they have less chance of being deported. Depending on the changing legislation we could cautiously say that there have been patterns in the choice of destination and children use their social capital to decide where to go, depending on where they suppose they can have more chances to stay.

This mobility directly affects the research, because sometimes the children disappear, meaning that it is difficult to keep long term contact. It can also happen that they suddenly re-appear again. New technologies can facilitate these pursuits, because some of the children use Internet or have a mobile phone. But with others there is no way I can contact them (just the streets and the contact with other children who might know them) Bloch (2007) found a similar result in a survey she did with Zimbabweans in the United Kingdom and in South Africa. With those in the UK an Internet survey worked perfectly fine whereas in the rural areas of South Africa with less educated respondents this method did not work out (Bloch, 2007). In some cases they had ways to contact me, but not the other way around. Sometimes contact was lost with a boy and suddenly months or even years later he appeared again in my life. The most significant example was a boy who I met five times between Barcelona and Tangier. He was deported several times, and without having any way of contacting each other we met informally at five different occasions in his life, first in Barcelona, then in Tangier, after in Barcelona again and another two times in Tangier, always in a casual meeting. To avoid these interruptions I used techniques highlighted by social networks practices, but even in these cases reality is more powerful than methodology and chance or luck becomes an important part of the research.

The double role: Anthropologist and social worker

The presence of the ethnographer is never neutral as one always has a role while doing participant observation. In my case, I used my double role: anthropologist and social educator. I combined the research with a current job as social educator with young immigrants in the city hall of Manresa, a city about 63 kilometres from Barcelona. This job had given me a lot of knowledge about the Foreigners Law, the protection system and the welfare system among others. It had also given me the opportunity to work with different types of children and families and get to know more about the origin situations. I do not work with unaccompanied minors, as a social educator I see only a few cases per year, but I can have the perspective of working inside the system on the one hand and researching from the outside on the other. I can really apply the classical double glance proposed so clearly by Levi-Strauss (1958/92) half a century ago: a distant analytical approach. On the other hand the critique from applied anthropology has highlighted the double perspective of working from the inside (see for example Foster 1969).

When I met people outside my job as social educator I told them that I was a social educator by formation, but that being with them was not part of my work, I was also a researcher, interested in the human rights perspective. Once clarifying this point, I used the information I had about the law, the protection system, and the resources, which I thought could help them. For me the participant observation was not a way to become a member of the group, which, due to my status as a Catalan woman, I think was impossible, but because I wanted to share some of the information that could be useful for them. In reverse they gave me information that was useful to me. The information I gave them was always general information, not related to private cases, which could infringe the law of personal confidentiality. I used this method not just with the children, but also with some of the families and other informants. Usually after I knew better what they already knew or what their opinions were about the law, the protection system, etc.

For me working as a social worker was not just a methodological tool of getting information; it was an ethical and moral choice. As they are opening to me a part of their private lives, I think it is fair to give them back part of the information I have. On the other hand, in doing so I create stronger ties with them, and I have more opportunities to collect more trustworthy information. This technique is also used in other research with street children. Lucchini (1999) for example also used the double role as social educator and researcher while interviewing street children in Brazil. I started my fieldwork with participant observation and collecting information in informal ways (without recording or even writing in a note book). Once I got a confidence relation I asked them if they agreed to record an interview. All the information in recorded interviews was contrasted with other information I had collected (information from informal conversations, from participant observation, from other sources such as protection system, friends, etc.). It was the complementation of all the different techniques of data collection that give me a useful and more precise overview of the phenomena.

Mistrust on the side of the children

When we're researching people at the margins, we have to face the fact that they will be suspicious of our research. They may misunderstand sometimes who we are or what we want. In the case of my research, it was not easy to win their trust. They sometimes thought I was a journalist or working for the secret police. Besides, a difficulty I faced during data collection was that most of the children operate in groups. It is thus not only about gaining trust from one child, but often from the group. Some of the boys used to leave when I approached the group they were joining. It took me more time to get information from them, or even on them, sometimes I couldn't get into contact with some boys. I remember a group of five in the beginning of my research that were deciding if I was a secret police, a journalist, or what I wanted from them. The beginnings are difficult, but then, as more children get to know you, as more families get to know you, it becomes easier to win their trust. Sometimes, getting to know their neighbourhood can also help to forge relations.

The mistrust was bigger, when the children had had previous bad experiences, for example with social educators. Also, the more time spent in the streets, away from the protection system, the bigger the suspicion was, and the difficulty of contacting and obtaining information from them. We can find the same situation or even worse when they have been sent back to Morocco, and they keep returning. The larger the spiral of coming and being sent back, the larger the difficulty to win their trust, they don't want to have contact with persons they link up with 'the system'. The only way I could deal with this was to have patience. It just did not work to try to push them to give me information.

Vulnerability of minors and careful handling of their irregular status

Socially, minors are one of the most vulnerable groups of society; in this case, this vulnerability increases by the fact that they are also persons in an 'irregular administrative situation', i.e. what is commonly called: illegal immigrants. When they arrive all of them are in irregular administrative situations, later on we can find them in different situations depending in how the administration responds to their demands. For that reason, I must be very meticulous with the kind of information I might give in articles or reports, making sure that I will not harm them, or put them in danger. The administration might be suspicious of the information I could produce, even more because I've been critical about the job of the administration and its results (Empez 2005). My position is that when the information is not relevant for the research it is better to avoid mentioning it. Sometimes ethnographers want to describe all the practices they think they have discovered, they may feel proud of collecting and obtaining information that is unknown to most people. But we must be very cautious in doing that. When we are talking about population at the margins, people that find themselves in a weak position we must be very cautious how we deal with the information they provide to us.

Conclusion

In this chapter I have analyzed the difficulties of doing fieldwork with unaccompanied minors in Barcelona, such as finding them and getting in contact with them. I talked about the mobility of the children, doing research in a transnational context, my double role as an anthropologist and social educator; the mistrust I faced from the children and the vulnerability of the minors in 'irregular administrative situations'. Also I raised the issue of ethical considerations that must be considered in order to try to not harm these children. But, even when in this chapter I have commented on the difficulties, I should also pay attention to the advantages of using this approach. Combining both the transnational and the ethnographic theories make it possible to better understand the effects of international migration dynamics for the actors involved. Studies in the field of migration should analyze people's lives in the transnational context and not divide people's lives between origin and destination. Using the case of unaccompanied minors from Morocco to Spain, I showed that changes in the Spanish Foreigners Law produce changes in the patterns of migration back in Morocco. Also sentimentally, some boys feel that they are the ones who had more opportunities to succeed in the migratory process, but even if they have travelled unaccompanied, they mentally have brought with them their families, with the duties, obligations and feelings. Their move will affect not just their own lives, but also the lives of the rest of their families. In current ethnographies our sense of time and space therefore needs to be updated accordingly.

Notes

1 EU Council Resolution 97/C 221/03 of 26 June 1997 on unaccompanied minors who are nationals of third countries.
2 Spain is divided by Autonomous Communities and Catalonia is one of them.
3 http://www.peretarres.org/daphneconred/estudi/index.html.
4 http://www.unhchr.ch/html/menu3/b/25.htm.
5 Free translation of: Artículo 92.5. '*Transcurridos nueve meses desde que el menor haya sido puesto a disposición de los servicios competentes de protección de menores, de acuerdo con el apartado 2, y una vez intentada la repatriación con su familia o al país de origen, si esta no hubiera sido posible, se procederá a otorgarle la autorización de residencia a la que se refiere la Ley orgánica 4/2000, de 11 de enero (. . .)*'.
6 That stay was funded by the Max Planck Institute of Demographic Research (MPIDR) in Rostock, Germany.

Bibliography

Bloch, A. (2007), 'Methodological Challenges for National and Multi-sited Comparative Survey Research', *Journal of Refugee Studies*, 20 (2): 230–247.
Capdevila, M. & M. Ferrer (2003), 'Els menors estrangers indocumentats no acompanyats' (MEINA). *Justicia i Societat* 24. Barcelona: Centre d'Estudis Jurídics i Formació Especialitzada.
Capdevila, M. (2001), *Menors al Carrer: la decepció d'un somni: una aproximació a la realitat del menor immigrat sol.* Barcelona: Pleniluni.
Con RED (2005), *Rutas de pequeños sueños: Los menores migrantes no acompañados en Europa.* Barcelona: Fundación Pere Tarrés.
Duran, F.J. (2007), 'Las administraciones públicas ante los menores extranjeros no acompañados: entre la represión y la protección'. *Revista electrónica de la Facultad de derecho de la Universidad de Granada.* http://www.refdugr.com/ documentos/articulos/4.pdf.

Empez, N. (2007), 'Social construction of neglect: the case of unaccompanied minors from Morocco to Spain'. *Working Paper* WP 2007-07. Rostock: Max Plank Institute of Demographic Research (MPIDR).

Empez, N. (2005), 'Menores No Acompañados en situación de exclusion social', in: T. Fernandez Garcia & J. Garcia Molina (eds.), *Multiculturalidad y educación: teorías, ámbitos y practices*: 314–333.

Foster, G. (1969), *Applied Anthropology*. The little brown series in Anthropology. Boston: Little Brown.

Hopkins, P. (2008), 'Ethical issues in research with unaccompanied asylum-seeking children', *Children's Geographies* 6 (1): 37–48.

Jiménez, A.M. (2006), 'Donde quiebra la protección: las reagrupaciones familiares sin garantías', *Estudios de derecho Judicial* 104: 53–76.

Jiménez, A.M, A. Bargach & E.A. Jiménez (2005), 'El reto de los menores e(in)migrantes', *Revista de derecho migratorio y extranjería* 9: 259–253.

Jiménez, A.M. & A. Ramírez (eds.) (2005), *Las otras migraciones: la emigración de menores marroquíes no acompañados a España*. Madrid: Akal.

Jiménez, A.M & D. Lorente (2004), *Menores en las fronteras: de los retornos efectuados sin garantías a menores marroquíes y de los malos tratos sufridos*. Madrid: SOS Racismo.

Larranga, M. (1999), 'Menors Immigrats sols o desemparats', *Fundació Jaume Bofill*, issue 32.

Lévis Strausse, C. (1992), *Antropología Estructural*, Buenos Aires: Paidos.

Lucchini, R. (1999), *Niño de la calle. Identidad, sociabilidad, droga*. Madrid: Los libros de la frontera.

Monresal, P. (1996), *Antropología y pobreza urbana*. Madrid: Los libros de la catarata.

Monteros, S. (2006), 'De Menores a Sujetos: Los Menores No Acompañados como Agentes de su Proceso Migratorio', in: *Catalogo de buenas pracicas para la inclusión*. Cruz Roja Española. http://practicasinclusion.org/ media/ 0504_Men_Agent_Proc_Mig.pdf.

Park, E.R. (1972), *The Crowd and the Public and Other Essays*. Chicago: University of Chicago Press.

Turner, R.H (eds.) (1967), *Robert Park on Social Control and Collective Behaviour: selected papers*. Chicago: University of Chicago Press.

Park. E.R., E.W. Burgess & R.D. Mc Kenzie (1925), *The City*. Chicago: University of Chicago Press.

Quiroga, V. (2003), *Els petits harraga. Menors Immigrats Irregulars No Acompanyats d'origen Marroquí a Catalunya*. Tesis doctoral. Departament d'Antropología Social. Tarragona: Universitat Rovira i Virgili.Quiroga.

Quiroga, V. (2002), 'Atenció als menors immigrats. Colaboració Catalunya – Marroc'. *Fundació Jaume Bofill*, issue 26.

Senovilla, D. (2007), *Situación y Tratamiento de los Menores Extranjeros No Acompañados en Europa*. Observatorio Internacional de Justicia Juvenil (OIJJ).

Síndic el defensor de les persones (2006), *Informe i recomanacions: La situació dels menors immigrats sols*. http://www.sindic.cat/es/page.asp?id=105.

Thomas, W. I. & F. Znanickci (1918), *The Polish Peasant in Europe and America. Monography of an Immigrant Group*. Boston: Boston University.

Index